"By their fruits shall ye know them."

Faith and Edward Deming Andrews on the lawn of their Shaker Farm in 1959.

FRUITS OF THE SHAKER TREE OF LIFE

*Memoirs of Fifty Years
of Collecting and Research*

Edward Deming Andrews

Faith Andrews

THE BERKSHIRE TRAVELLER PRESS
STOCKBRIDGE, MASSACHUSETTS

Selected Titles from The Berkshire Traveller Press:

Country Inns and Back Roads

Shop Drawings of Shaker Furniture and Woodenware, Volume I

Shop Drawings of Shaker Furniture and Woodenware, Volume II

Forthcoming:

Shop Drawings of Shaker Iron and Tinware

Library of Congress Cataloging in Publication Data
Andrews, Edward Deming, 1894-1964
    Fruits of the Shaker tree of life.

    1. Shakers.   I. Andrews, Faith, joint author.
II.   Title.
BX9771.A64   1975   289.8   75-33901

ISBN 0-912944-32-3

This book is dedicated to our children and grandchildren.
May they, too, know the "gift of inspiration"
and partake of the fruits of the tree of life.

BOOKS BY THE AUTHORS

The Community Industries of the Shakers. The University of the State of New York, 1932.

Shaker Furniture:The Craftsmanship of an American Communal Sect. Yale University Press, New Haven, Connecticut, 1937. Reprinted by Dover Publications, New York, 1950.

The Gift to be Simple: Songs, Dances and Rituals of the American Shakers. J.J. Augustin, New York, 1940. Reprinted by Dover Publications, New York, 1962.

The People Called Shakers: A Search for the Perfect Society. Oxford University Press, New York, 1954. Enlarged edition, including an Appendix of Notes, Dover Publications, New York, 1963.

Religion in Wood: A Book of Shaker Furniture. Indiana University Press, Bloomington, Indiana, 1966.

Visions of the Heavenly Sphere: A Study in Shaker Religious Art. Published for The Henry Francis du Pont Winterthur Museum by The University Press of Virginia, Charlottesville, Virginia, 1969.

Work and Worship: The Economic Order of the Shakers. New York Graphic Society, Greenwich, Connecticut. 1974.

A comprehensive list of fifty articles, essays and pamphlets, covering all aspects of the Shaker culture may be found in: *Shaker: Furniture and Objects from the Faith and Edward Deming Andrews Collections,* published for the Renwick Gallery of the National Collection of Fine Arts by the Smithsonian Institution Press, City of Washington, 1973.

ACKNOWLEDGEMENT

I followed the suggestion of our oldest grandson, Edward Deming Andrews II, that publication of our memoirs be directed to the Berkshire Traveller Press in Stockbridge, Massachusetts. I am indebted to him for his suggestion. Also, I am grateful to the staff of the Press for their rare understanding of the manuscript and tireless efforts to meet its demands.

F.A.

FOREWORD

This memoir is a record of the many years of our collecting and personal relationships with the people called Shakers. We realize, more and more, that we have been privileged to be among the last witnesses of a way of life, a distinct American culture, that is gradually but inevitably receding into the past. And as witnesses—or "instruments" to use a Shaker term—we feel that it is important to set down the day-by-day incidents, our reactions to certain experiences, the pleasures of search and research, as well as the disappointments and obstacles which accompanied our effort to document a whole culture. Much historical writing is based on the discovery and interpretation of existing sources, printed and manuscript. We used them, too, of course. But it was our good fortune to enter into the actual life of a secluded people, and to receive from them, fresh and direct, what they had to give, of spiritual as well as material "gifts." Precious were these fruits of the Shaker tree of life.

Edward Deming Andrews
Faith Andrews

CONTENTS

LIST OF ILLUSTRATIONS

Illustrations marked with an asterisk (*) are reprinted through the courtesy of The Henry Francis du Pont Winterthur Museum, The Edward Deming Andrews Memorial Shaker Collection.

THE SHAKERS

In the middle of the eighteenth century Ann Lee, the unlettered daughter of a blacksmith in Manchester, England, left the textile mills of the manor, where she had been employed since early childhood, to join a small Quaker society which had come under the influence of the French Prophets or Camisards. Her motivation was essentially one of protest—against misunderstandings at home, the indifference of the established church, the intolerable working conditions in the factories, and the squalid poverty of the slums. The Quaker society was even more of a haven when, a few years later, she was given in an unwanted marriage to one Abraham Stanley, another blacksmith, by whom she had four children, all of whom died in infancy.

In the tradition of the heretical Prophets, members of the society indulged in forms of ecstatic worship which aroused increasingly the opposition of the neighborhood. Ann and others were arrested for disturbing the Sabbath. In prison, according to her testimony, she received revelations in which she was divinely commissioned, as the person in whom the Christ spirit had appeared the second time, to consummate the work that Jesus had begun. After her release, by virtue of a strong personality and an inspired sense of mission, she assumed leadership in the society, and as the "Mother" of a new dispensation, started to preach her strange gospel. In it certain Quaker principles persisted: the doctrine of inner light, the refusal to bear arms or swear oaths, plainness of speech and dress. Others were clearly the result of her own experience. Salvation, she taught, could be attained only by separation from a sinful world, the world of private property and contention, the world of carnal "lust" and marriage. To be regenerated, one must rise above the plane of generation. She had a resplendent vision of a New Jerusalem, a restoration of the primitive Christian church.

Misunderstood and persecuted in her native land, Ann, with eight followers, emigrated to America in 1774. After a two-year interval in and around New York, the little band of "Shaking Quakers" settled in the wilderness of Niskeyuna (later called Watervliet) near Albany. The next four years were spent improving the land, planting crops, building shelters, and prayerfully waiting for the opportunity to open their testimony. This came in the guise of a New Light Baptist revival at New Lebanon, New York, and adjacent towns, in the aftermath of which certain disillusioned leaders, hearing of the Shaker sect, its dynamic leader and its wondrous worship in dance and song, came to accept her message that the millennium for which they had longed had already had its inception in her wilderness home.

The year was 1780. Contact had been made with an indigenous religious movement, with American life and people. From a small beginning the ferment spread until, aided both by missionary effort and persecution, the millennial gospel established itself in many parts of New England and eastern New York. After the death of Mother Ann in 1784, her chief disciple, James Whittaker, laid the foundations for a communitarian society, and in 1786, a year before he died, dedicated the first meeting house at New Lebanon. The work of organizing the church into a United Society with a written covenant, "family" orders, trades and prescribed socio-religious practices, was entrusted to Whittaker's successor, "Father" Joseph Meacham, a native of Enfield, Connecticut, who had been a lay preacher of the New Lights.

When Meacham died in 1796 the Shaker order had become fully established. Besides the two in New York state communities had been organized at Enfield, at Shirley, Harvard, Tyringham and Hancock in Massachusetts, at Alfred and New Gloucester (Sabbathday Lake) in Maine, and at Canterbury and Enfield in New Hampshire. After the turn of the century, again as the result of an awakening in other denominations—the great Southern and Western Revival—Shaker colonies were founded in Ohio, at Union Village, Watervliet, White Water and North Union (Shaker Heights); in Kentucky, at Pleasant Hill and South Union; and in Indiana, at Busro or West Union. In 1826 the last society to be established (with the exception of two short-lived, late century colonies in Florida and Georgia) was founded at Sodus Bay, New York, moving to Groveland in the same state, ten years later. The movement reached its numerical zenith about mid-century, with eighteen branches and some six thousand members. The longest-lived of American experiments in communitarianism, and in many respects the most productive, it still survives in two places, Canterbury and Sabbathday Lake, with about two score covenant members.

The Shakers lived for a principle, subordinating individual interests to the causes for which their church stood. The principle itself, for those who joined the order, was a selective agent. Yet it may be said that in serving the church every true convert came to realize his or her best self, with personality accentuated rather than diminished in the process. Attired alike, subject to the same ordinances and same routine, the Believers, as depicted in early group stereographs, seem like placid and depersonalized human beings. Intimate acquaintance, however, belies that impression. Many sisters and brethren we have known, and many others whose lives are recorded in Shaker literature, were individuals in their own right, humble and unworldly, sometimes "singular", but always forthright in their convictions and earnest in their search for rectitude. Character was molded by discipline and commitment to the purposes to which they had voluntarily consecrated their possessions and talents. Like their workmanship, they tended to conform, in outward appearance and inner spirit, to a common pattern; but however circumscribed the culture may seem, it still allowed for self-expression and differentiation in the labor of their lands.

Basically, the values for which they lived were human values. "We believed we were debtors to God, in relation to each other, and all men, to improve our time and talents in this Life, in that manner in which we might be most useful." So read their covenant. To labor was to pray. In building, their concern was light and heat, space and simplicity, convenience and health. Their care of children and the aged and infirm was humane and advanced for their time. They opened their doors to the poor and the homeless, their purse to the victims of fire, disease and famine. In their barns one found, placarded on the wall, the admonition that "A man of kindness to his beast is kind." The soil they looked upon as an element to be "redeemed." The confessional was an institution for spiritual guidance. Leadership was based on character and service. Their mode of address was "More love, brother." "More love, sister." With moving testimonial, while spirits watched, gently they laid their dead to rest.

FRUITS OF THE SHAKER

TREE OF LIFE

I

BEGINNINGS

When people ask us, "How did you first become interested in the Shakers?" the real explanation is so involved that by the time it is completed, the questioner has lost interest. It is always difficult to tell just when and how an interest originates, and what makes it grow.

Faced with the question, we sometimes resorted to the following fable. When David and Ann, our children, were aged eight and six respectively, they occupied separate bedrooms in a large Victorian house in Pittsfield, Massachusetts. When the lights were out they liked to talk, calling from room to room, postponing sleep as long as possible. Once Ann asked her brother how lions first became man-eaters. David, not hesitant to exhibit his superior knowledge of such things—he was going through the stage of collecting bugs, butterflies, fossils, etc.—had, as usual, a ready answer: "Well, Ann, you see it was like this. A lion once saw a man, tasted him, liked him and kept right on eating him."

Naturally the story puzzled and never quite satisfied the inquirers. More satisfactory was our account of an incident that occurred one cool September afternoon in 1923. After a day in the countryside looking for old furniture, glass, china and pewter, we were driving home in our Model T along the route which, leading from the eastern foot of the Taconic range to our Pittsfield home, passed by the old Hancock Shaker village where "two roads diverged in a yellow wood." Why did we diverge? We had heard about the delicious Shaker bread. We decided to stop to inquire if it could be bought, and when the basement door in the large brick dwelling was opened to us, we were greeted by the aroma of fresh-baked loaves.

A soft-voiced Shaker sister welcomed us warmly. We bought two loaves of bread. And in the long clean "cook-room" we saw much besides: a trestle table, benches, rocking chairs, built-in cupboards, cooking arches, all beautiful in their simplicity. Later, eating the bread, we knew that our appetite would not be satisfied with bread alone. In the words of an old Shaker song, we had tasted of "the crums of Heaven."

The acquisition of our first chair was a memorable experience. Though born and raised within a few miles of the Hancock Shakers, neither of us knew much more about them than the current gossip that they were a "peculiar" sect. We had never heard that they made their own furniture. No one had ever collected it. No one knew the history of their chair industry, nor when and by whom the furnishings of the community dwellings and shops were produced. The Shakers themselves took their craftsmanship for granted. Yet here, we came to discover, was a distinct school of joinery and industry about which nothing had been written. When we purchased those loaves of bread and that simple three-slat side chair with its woven seat, we did not know that we were taking the first steps in a work which would open up vast avenues of research. We did not know that as time went on we would become deeply involved in the attempt to preserve, in words as in objects, a richly productive strain in American history. It was to become a lifework.

As collector-dealers in colonial and post-colonial artifacts—a hobby pursued for gain as well as pleasure during summer vacations from teaching and graduate study—there was often a need to dispose of some Shaker acquisitions to those few discriminating customers who sensed their unique quality. It was not long, however, before we became loath to part with what the Shakers had been willing to sell, even though our means were slim. Occasionally we would sell what we thought was an inferior piece in order to purchase a better example. But this was not very helpful, for so little *was* inferior. The assembling of a collection was indeed a luxury enterprise and, for awhile, one that was unrecognized.

What we needed was encouragement in the field of interpretation. And therein lies another tale.

As subscribers to *The Magazine Antiques,* whose editorial office was then in Boston, we knew that the founding editor, Homer Eaton Keyes, was publishing original studies on various phases of American folk art and craftsmanship, that he was encouraging scholarship wherever it emerged, and opening the magazine freely to new discoveries in a hitherto neglected field. We wrote him about our work and had lunch with him in Boston.

Our next meeting with Mr. Keyes was in New Haven. In our Chapel Street apartment there were several early American pieces: a slant-top desk, two four-poster beds, a tavern table, a cherry dropleaf table, two Windsors and a bannister-back arm chair. We had brought from the country one Shaker chair, but we had given it to a friend and neighbor.

This was in the fall of 1927. We had written again to Mr. Keyes—who now had moved his offices to New York—inviting him to dinner. The reply was warm and encouraging. He wanted to know more about the Shakers and see examples, or at least illustrations, of their crafts-manship. He would be happy to come.

On the memorable evening of his call the children had been tucked in for the night, the table laid, and the Shaker chair borrowed from the neighbor. To honor our visitor, a native of New Hampshire, the dinner was a New England one—but I doubt whether we knew what we were eating. The talk ranged far and wide, and for the first time we got a needed perspective on our work, seeing it in terms of American art and history as a whole. The simple tilting chair, serving as a symbol of all Shaker furniture, was all that was needed to convince our guest that here was a unique native school of craftsmanship that should be better known. So, as he left to catch a late train back to New York, he asked us to submit an article for his magazine. Published in the August 1928 issue, it was our first description and interpretation of Shaker furniture, the first in a series in the magazine, and the beginning of our serious research which was ultimately to embrace all phases of the life and work of the Believers. It was from Homer Keyes that we received the priceless gift of faith. On that autumn evening our interest became a calling.

Shortly before this another experience served as a test of how much we really cared about our Shaker things. In the cellar of a house which formerly was a brethren's shop at the Second family in West Pittsfield, we found two Shaker trestle tables—abandoned, forgotten. We bought them gladly. When we showed our find to our families, they did not share our enthusiasm, but when we sold them at a considerable profit, they were impressed. Then, it may have been a year later, we wanted a trestle table for our own use and could not find one. (The Shaker communities had been combed long before our time for such tables, which had infiltrated into the antiques market as colonial pieces.) So we tried to trace our two. The collector who had bought one would not part with it. The other was owned by a dealer in Westfield, where we journeyed in trepidation lest it had been sold. But no, there it was, on a dark side porch almost obscured by other furniture. We bought it back, this cherished piece, for almost the sum we had received for the sale of the two. In 1928, when our article appeared in *The Magazine Antiques,* one of its illustrations was the twice-bought table we had almost lost.

We were beginning to learn and to keep what was good. There was no question in our minds when we came across our next trestle board. At the West family in New Lebanon, New York, nestled in the woods at the foot of the mountain, there was an old stone grist mill built, according to the end-irons under the north gable, in 1824. The overshot wheel was in ruins, but the mill itself, with one remaining family dwelling, was structurally sound. The property had passed from Shaker

Twenty-foot trestle table

hands into the possession of a New Yorker who manufactured drugs. He had remodeled the house, and was engaged in some pharmaceutical venture on the third floor of the mill.

It was an unlikely repository of artifacts, but it was about the only building in the New Lebanon settlement we had not explored. So one autumn day we drove down the narrow lane which was its outlet to the world. No one was at home, but the door of the mill was open, an invitation which could not be resisted. On the ground floor, a dimly lit cavern, there was some long disused machinery. There was nothing on the second floor. But after climbing the wide open stairway to the top story, we saw, standing along the north wall under the windows, a magnificent Shaker trestle dining table, twenty feet long! Its top was coated with grease and grime and littered with dirty bottles. Someone, to raise its height, had put bed-rollers on its three arched supports or legs. But it had its original dark red finish and was as sound as the day it was made. Correspondence with the owner followed. He had no use for the piece, and we were glad to accept his price, plus carting, which was no easy matter.

We have always thought it was fate which led us to these rare tables. Certainly that was the case with another find. One morning in the early summer of 1956 we started out from our Richmond farm on the hunt for old furniture. We had no particular destination, no special piece in mind, though we told each other how wonderful it would be if we could find a cupboard, an early chest of drawers, or best of all, a trestle table. We drove to Canaan, New York, passed the Berkshire Industrial Farm on Route 22, and had gone about a mile on the road to Albany when we saw, coming towards us and traveling at high speed, a touring car on the top of which was strapped what was unmistakably a Shaker trestle! Turning around as fast as we could, we pursued our quarry along the highway, far exceeding the speed limit and despairing lest we be outdistanced. But a truck on a long curve slowed the other car down. We got in back of it and kept honking. Finally the driver, fearing perhaps that he was losing his load, pulled his car to the side of the road.

He was an Ohio dealer. The table—it was indeed a superb Shaker piece, all curly maple—had come from the vicinity of the Union Village, Ohio, community. But our hearts sank when he told us it had been promised to another dealer in the Connecticut Valley. He wasn't sure whether this person would take it, however, and gave us the name and address of the consignee.

The next morning we got in touch with the Connecticut dealer. He had bought the table—why wouldn't he—but it had not been resold, though two customers, both interested in Shaker furniture, were going to look at it that afternoon. However, if we said then and there we would take it, he would give us an option. The price, in four figures, was far beyond anything we had ever paid for a Shaker piece. But not to have it, after all the suspense, would have cost more. The upshot was that we journeyed over the back roads that fine sunny morning, and by noon the prize was tied to the top of our own car.

It was true collector's luck. Five minutes later on the Albany road and we would have lost what we set out to find that summer day.

II

THE SHAKERS AND THE ESSENES

One of the values of historical study is that the pursuit of one theme leads the scholar into related avenues and by-paths of research. In our case a specialized interest broadened to include a desire to learn about other American communitarian societies: Amana, Harmony, Zoar, Bethel, Aurora, Icaria, Oneida and the rest. It stimulated interest in the Mormons, the Quakers, the Camisards, the Waldenses, the Albigenses and other dissenting sects; and in the monastic orders and their fountainhead, the primitive Christian church. A knowledge of revivalism about the Methodists, Baptists, and Presbyterians in the early years of the republic was essential background for understanding of the Shaker movement. So was the literature of early American travel, invention and industry, folk art, folk song and domestic architecture, spiritualism and psychic research, state laws relating to religious societies, and so on. In various measure and with pertinent allusion, all bore on the subject of our chief concern. All knowledge, we discovered, is interrelated.

However, there was one sect, an ancient one, whose beliefs and practices were in many respects so like those of the Shakers as to invite special study. The first reference we encountered to this sect was in a catalogue of medicinal plants, barks, roots, seeds, flowers and select powders raised and prepared by the Shakers at New Lebanon, in which C.S. Rafinesque, the Franco-American botanist, observed that "the best medical gardens in the United States are those established by the communities of Shakers or modern Essenes, who cultivate and collect a great variety of medical plants." Allusions to the Hebrew anchorites who lived near the Dead Sea in the second century before Christ occurred in the works of Hepworth Dixon, the English scholar who greatly admired the Shakers, and in Charles Edson Robinson's series of papers on *The Shakers and their Homes.* With the discovery of the Dead Sea scrolls, including the "Manual of Discipline" of the Essenes, more light was thrown on this pre-Christian cult. The content of the Manual "tallies almost exactly"* with the summary of Essenian practice given by Flavius Josephus, the Jewish historian, who had been the chief source of information on the Essenes. The discovery of the scrolls, following earlier scattered references, made us curious to know more about those herbalists and seedsmen. It was a source of wonder that two such experiments in religious communitarianism, separated so widely in time and space, could evolve such similar patterns of culture. We are reminded here of the many similarities between the monastic Rule of St. Benedict and the Millennial Laws of the Shakers.

Both societies believed in common ownership of property, in the principle that one should give up all one's possessions on entering into the sacred fellowship. In both cases the commitment was a gradual one, proceeding from a novitiate where property and family ties were retained, through an intermediate order (a Junior Order in the case of the Shakers, an "approacher" with the Essenes), and finally complete renunciation of the world and complete consecration to the cause. Josephus records the fact that there was a branch of the Essenian sect which allowed the members to marry. Such a branch would be comparable to the first stage of membership in the Shaker society. In this connection it should be noted that the former order was otherwise for males only, whereas the latter welcomed both men and women, who were accorded equal rights and responsibilities and lived and worshipped together, though under strict "separation acts."

Both societies were celibate, mortifying the lusts of the flesh, and suffering persecution as the result of the doctrine. However, though they renounced marriage for themselves, neither order, on principle, condemned wedlock in the world. According to Josephus, the Essenes recognized the fact that if everyone declined to marry "the whole race would very quickly die out." Similarly Ann Lee, the founder of the Shakers counselled for all who were unable "to take up a full cross, and part with every gratification of the flesh," that they "take wives in a lawful manner, and cleave to them only; and raise up a lawful posterity, and be perpetual servants to your families: for of all lustful gratifications that is the least sin." In both cases the institutions were perpetuated partly by conversions but chiefly by the adoption of children from the world.

To further the concept of purity, both sects secluded themselves in colonies separated from the world—"since contact with anyone who did not practice their beliefs made them impure." The ascetic quality of their lives did not prevent either society, however, from practicing a rare benevolence not only to one another, the sick and aged in particular, but

---

* Edmund Wilson, "The Scrolls of the Dead Sea," *The New Yorker*, May 14, 1955.

to the world they had forsaken. In this connection, it may be noted that as the alleged result of the purity, security and regularity of their lives, members of both sects lived beyond the normal span. Josephus reported that most of the Essenes lived to be over a hundred!

There were other similarities. Swearing of oaths was a desecration. "Any word of theirs," Josephus wrote of the Essenes, "had more force than an oath." In similar vein, Richard McNemar, in his *General Inquiry* on the Shakers, told the world that:

> In civil courts we hold no seat,
> Nor great ones with high titles greet;
> We lift no hand, we kiss no book,
> To sanction anything we've spoke;
> Nor need we swear at all forsooth,
> Because we speak the simple truth.*

Secrets were also outlawed. One could not give presents to relatives in the world without permission of the superiors. Temperance was the rule in drinking and eating. Scrupulous attention was paid to cleanliness. Slavery was condemned and politics shunned.

Worship, with the Shakers as with the Essenes, was marked by prophecies and divine revelations. The Believers were spiritualists, holding communion with their Father-Mother God, with Jesus and Mother Ann, with their dear departed ones. The Essenes held that spiritual intercourse with God was a sign, the "last stage," of perfection on earth. There was no ordained ministry in either order; though there were priests or elders selected for their spiritual gifts, any member could read or speak in meeting. In the doctrine of both churches the body was held to be corruptible but the soul imperishable.

The parallel holds for the daily routine. Division of labor was the practice. Dressed in the plainest of garments, the Hebrew brethren engaged in pursuits strikingly similar to those of the Shakers; they were beekeepers, shepherds and cowherds, cultivators of flowers, herbs and seeds, artisans and craftsmen. In marketing products, we find the counterpart of the Shaker deacon or trustee in the Essenian steward, who did all the buying and selling and handled all accounts. For both the Old World and New World communities life was a busy but tranquil and orderly one, broken only by the punctual meals, the apportioned labors, the periods of worship and of rest. With a grace before and after their silent meals, the devotees of these faiths thanked God for their blessings. Their whole life was a sacrament.

---

* Richard McNemar, *A Concise Answer to the General Inquiry, Who, or What are the Shakers.* Union Village, Ohio. 1868.

III

HERB LORE

In the 1950's we had an exhibition at the Berkshire Garden Center in Stockbridge, Massachusetts, covering the Shaker Herb industry. It was a delightful and fitting place for such a display. Through lectures and audience response we became aware of a genuine interest in the propagation and use of herbs.

At the request of the Berkshire Garden Center we wrote a brochure entitled: "Shaker Herbs and Herbalists." It was printed by Carl Purington Rollins of Yale University Press in 1959. Again through the courtesy of the Berkshire Garden Center, Inc. it is reprinted here as a reminder of another important Shaker contribution.   F.A.

The Shakers were the first people in this country to grow herbs on a large scale for the pharmaceutical market. Medicinal plants, chiefly wild herbs, were gathered at New Lebanon, N.Y., as early as 1800. Excepting what was sold for the purpose of purchasing other medicines, these were used by the physicians at home, but as the demand from the new world grew greater, an industry developed there, and in other branches of the United Society of Believers, which became one of the most lucrative of Shaker enterprises.

To meet this demand—which was due in part to the "spurious and adulterated drugs" on the market—"psychic gardens" were laid out at New Lebanon abut 1820, and two brethren from the Church family, "Dr." Eliab Harlow and Garrett Lawrence, undertook a more "scientific manner of conducting the business, especially as to the seasons of collection, varieties and methods of preparations."

The industry prospered from the first. It was not long before an extract business supplemented the sale of dried roots and herbs: in an early sales book of 1826-8 we find such items as sweet marjoram, sage, cow parsnip extract, digestive pills, cicuta extract, skunk cabbage root, extracts of hops and butternut, syrup of liverwort, eye water, bugle, belladonna, sarsaparilla, cohosh, princes pine, scullcap, lemon balm and stramonium leaves. By 1831 the reputation of Shaker herbs had become wide-spread: an entry in one day-book cites an order for a box of herbs from Paris, and another "for the own use of Rafinesque"— Prof. C.S. Raffinesque, the well known French-American botanist. In October of that year thirteen boxes of medicinal herbs were "delivered on board ship *Hannibal* in the port of New York—for Charles Whitlaw Botanist of London" ($895.65). Raffinesque was later to comment that "the best medical gardens in the United States are those established by the communities of Shakers, or modern Essenes." Canterbury and Enfield, N.H., Harvard and Hancock, Mass., Watervliet, N.Y., Enfield, Conn., New Gloucester, Maine, Union Village, Ohio, and other societies were developing the herb industries concurrently with that of the parent order at New Lebanon.

There the business was so active that a drying and pressing house was needed by 1832, and by 1833, if not before, the first catalogues were issued. The catalogue of 1833 is a slim 8-page pamphlet with pale green wrappers, published by Ashbel Stoddard in Hudson, N.Y. On the title-page is the couplet,

> "Why send to Europe's distant shores
> For plants which grow at our own doors?"—

one of the earliest instances, surely, of the will to make America more independent of foreign imports. By this time the New Lebanon Shakers were selling four thousand pounds of herbs and roots a year, an output which was to be quadrupled in the next eighteen years. Lebanon was the largest producer, with a considerable percentage of the 150 acres which, by 1860, were devoted to botanical uses in the United Society as a whole.

Glimpses into the day-by-day occupations of the herb gardens are afforded by many carefully kept journals. Here, for instance, is a page from the diary of an unknown Shaker brother, probably Jonathan Wood, who was assigned to the business during the Lawrence-Harlow regime.* The time is May, 1836:

16 M.　 I commence working in the medical Garden.
　　　　 Strange things! ! We scrape & level the ground
　　　　 north of the Alley & sow it to Sage..........

17 tues. We work on the South side of the Alley, &
　　　　 plough & scrape & fix a bed & sow it to white-
　　　　 root & summer savory & set out some Butten
　　　　 snakeroot. I continue ploughing east etc

18 W.　 We rake and sow a bed, some sweet basil &
　　　　 Foxglove & Moldaven Balm. . . . . . in the P.M.
　　　　 we set out some rose bushes

19 Th　 We continue working in the garden etc

20 Fr.　 Garrett (Lawrence) has a bad turn and I tend
　　　　 upon him besides ploughing the ground for

---

*In quotations from early manuscripts the original spelling and punctuation are retained.

peppermint & for I. Bates's willow slips. I.
Bates & Eliab Harlow set out the slips.

21 Sa   We set out the Hysop beside the alley & finish
fixing the Alley. Garret gits some better. . . . .

23 M.   We commence setting out catnep. . . . .

24 Tu   We finish setting out catnep & plough up the
Tanzy bed and set out some red rose bushes. . . . . . .

25 W   We transplant some lemon Balm & rake & fix a
bed & set out some Lobelia Sifilittica.

26 th   We set out the peppermint and Tanzy etc.

27 fr   Nothing done in the garden today I put up
some Extracts

28 Sa   We set out some chamomile & a row of Lovage
& mash Mallow, and sow three rows Poppys in
the P.M. We put some tan on the Alley, etc.etc.

30 M.   Garret & I clean out & put things in Order at
the drying house.

31 tu   . . . . I help I.B. & E.H. hoe out the horehound

In June this brother "assists Garrett about his Alterative syrup," transplants belladonna, "pouns" cicuta, picks it over for drying, and puts it in the kiln; in July he cuts sage, weeds out thyme and transplants foxglove; one day in September he "goes on the mountain with Betsy Bates and Lucy Clark after Bugle & skulcap and other herbs;" in October we find him grinding hellebore, lady's-slipper and slippery elm, gathering garden lettuce stalks. for extracts, and traveling to Watertown, N.Y. after wormwood. During the same period he is busy with other "chores," an exemplar of the Shaker belief that "variety of labor" was a source of pleasure as well as a means of improving time and talent. The diary has such entries as these:

Make preparations for making a closet in the drying house
Edge some boards and commence covering the cabin down
by the garden.
Go on the hill to work at the highway.
Commence building a flight of steps up the ledge.
Make a mitten han [wooden form for mending mittens] for
Sarah Fairchild.
Grind the guilotine for Eliab Harlow to cut herbs with
Help raise the new addition to the wash house.
Hang two gates acrost the Cow lane
Commence helping hay it.
Take care of Luther Copley who is sick with one of his turns
Commence cradling [wheat?] above the north orchard.
Run some Cherry bark through the bark mill
Help Francis Hocknell stiffen some hats
Go over to Hancock with some sisters to lern how to make
rie bread.
Help Daniel Crosman bucher the beaf.

"How similar to colonization in a new country, communal

association necessarily is," a Shaker elder (Giles B. Avery) once wrote, "that members of a community should be willing to turn a hand in any needed direction in order to render their best service in building up and sustaining the cause."

Wild herbs were often gathered to supplement those grown in the Shakers' own medical gardens. Another New Lebanon journal, commenced in 1841, records frequent trips into the countryside or to near-by towns where particular plants were known to be obtainable. The anonymous diarist, sometimes alone and sometimes in the company of brethren or sisters, went, for instance,

> to Whiting's Pond [Queechy Lake] for roots and herbs
> to Watervliet to dig mandrake roots
> to Lenox for some sweet fern
> to Greenbush after peach leaves
> to Lainsburrow [sic] after wormwood
> to Ghent after indigo root a kind of medical root
> to Pittsfield after sweet flag
> to Lenox mountain after crosswort
> to a place south of Whiting's Pond after red root
> to Washington to gather wild Lettice and Bone Set herbs
> to Lenox after Comfry roots
> to the North part of Richmount [Richmond] to gather
> some Skunk Cabbage Leaves
> to Sheffield after boneset
> to Canaan after cat tail flag, boneset and vervine
> [vervane] blue and white
> to Pittsfield after wintergreen

After the deaths of Garrett Lawrence in 1837 and Eliab Harlow in 1840, the herb industry at New Lebanon was conducted by Wood, Barnabus Hinckley and eventually by Edward Fowler, whom Benson J. Lossing, the American artist and historian, described as a "short, thick-set man of sixty, with ruddy, smiling face, upon every lineament of which is imprinted assurances of great integrity." In 1857, with this brother as his guide, Lossing visited (and later sketched) the herb house at New Lebanon, recording his impressions in the following words:

> "What pleasant odors come from this building, more than a hundred feet in length! They remind us of the 'spouse' in Solomon's Song who is likened unto a 'garden'—an 'orchard of pomegranate, with pleasant fruits, camphire with spikenard; spikenard and saffron; calamus and cinnamon, with all trees of frankincense; myrrh and aloes, with all the chief spices.' It is the Herbarium where almost every herb used in the *materia medica* is brought from their gardens and fields, and here dried, pressed and packed for market—seventy-five tons in the course of a year!"

The Herb-House, Mount Lebanon

Lossing must have been particularly interested in the technical phase of the industry, for he drew, and later, with his partner Barritt, engraved sketches of the apparatus used—the vacuum pan, the hydraulic press, crushing mill, powdering mill and laboratory—pictures which were to illustrate an article he subsequently published in *Harper's Monthly* (1857).

Brother Fowler's Letter Book for 1859-61, in which he posted all incoming correspondence for those years, documents the scope as well as the problems involved in this far-flung enterprise. Many of the letters came from California—San Francisco and Sacramento—little more than a decade after the discovery of gold had opened up that distant territory. There is considerable correspondence with Coleman's California Line, New York to San Francisco, "Dispatching regularly & promptly two to three Firstclass Clipper Ships per month" —ships named *David Crockett, Nabob* and *Skylark*, the latter a "great favorite with all California shippers." A large account was with the "Drug House of Charles Morrill" in San Francisco. From Victoria, Vancouver Island, Custis & Moore wrote, on March 14, 1860, that "we wish to open a trade with you and hope you will give us a liberal credit . . . This country is filling up very fast. There is a large immigration expected this year there is no doubt but that in five years it will be as important as California was five years ago." Early the next year a shipment of Shaker herbs and garden seeds arrived at Victoria on the ship *Sunshine*.

Damage to shipments was common. Some of the bundles on the

Sunshine were broken and seeds mixed. A New York underwriter reported to Fowler that ten bales of hops on the *Reynard* were damaged when the ship had to put back to Boston, "having been dismasted in a gale when only a few days out." Containers often arrived broken. Sometimes the powders were too dry or too wet. James Jackson, M.D. wrote from Melbourne, Australia that a barrel of slippery elm powder was adulterated: "instead of being miscellagenous it is a mealy substance, and American people here say it is about half Elm powder and half something else."

Inquiries came from every quarter. The Covent Garden Market in London asked about the lowest prices for henbane, hemlock, belladonna (deadly nightshade), belladonna leaves, dandelion, basil and podophyllin (Podophyllum, the Mayapple or mandrake). From W. W. Parker of Davenport, Iowa, came the report that he was entering the wholesale and retail drug business and wanted a large quantity of botanical preparations at a price which would enable him to compete with Chicago.

Two of the most interesting letters were from tradesmen in Wilkesboro, North Carolina, and St. Louis—interesting because they combined business with political observations on the eve of the Civil War. Thus, on October 29, 1860, J.H. and C.J. Cowles wrote from Wilkesboro: "The presidential election comes off tomorrow week and much anxiety is felt here for the result. We are *union men* but our people are not all so. If Lincoln is elected S. Carolina will try to break the union & God only knows what may be the result." And on Feb. 19, 1861, William L. Felix, of St. Louis, after concluding his order, wrote that "This city yesterday voted the unconditional Union ticket by 5000 majority and I think the whole state will be for the Union, thus all the border states have decided for the Union, and if our friends in Congress will be a little conciliatory we can be saved from disunion and leave the Cotton states to themselves and see how they will like it, we can live without them if they can without us . . . ." The crisis was already affecting the drug business of J.J. Merrill in that city: "I can hardly say what the prospect for getting roots here this year will be," he complains in a letter of May 18, 1861, "as there is so many of the population enlisted in the Army that there is an Increased demand for labor, [however] money is so very scarce that it will have a tendency to stimulate rooters to operate to raise it." The Civil War seriously depleted herb orders and all but wiped out the sale of Shaker garden seeds in the South and Southwest.

Though Shaker doctrine called for "separation from the world" and all worldly practices—marriage, private property, politics, war— it did not imply economic isolation, a policy which would have cut off their markets. From the first the deacons and trustees also bought from the world those manufactures and raw materials, including herbs, which they could not produce themselves. A substantial part of their pharmaceutical trade, both buying and selling, was with wholesalers. Much of it, however, was with small dealers near and far, and on occasion with individuals who carried on the ancient tradition of gathering "simples" for family or local use. Such a person was Horace Jennings, a pedlar of Searsburg, Vermont, who wrote to Brother Fowler in August, 1860:

> I learnt by a man geathering Hearbs for you
> you Bought Balmony [snakehead] Sculcap wake Robin etc
> I am gethering Some of these kinds I have of Balmony 300
> Pounds well Sorted & Dried in house on Racks what do you
> Pey for it Some was gethered in bud Some in blow I cannot
> make it look as well as Skulcap what is Evens Root worth . .
> Dwarf Elder is plenty on my rout wild Latice [lettuce]
> Pipsisaway Mountain Ash Sassafras etc . . My Balmony is
> Dry . . .

The record of daily routine of the Shaker journalists is often interspersed with personal observations—on the weather, on the sermons they heard in meeting, the songs and dances in which they participated, their work and its place in the scheme of things. Elisha Myrick, the herbalist at the Harvard, Mass. community, for example, frequently terminated the year's record with a bit of philosophy:

> The wheels of time by their increasing revolutions have brought
> us around to the close of another year. The earth has generously
> repaid man for his toil—nature gives abundantly to those who
> ask aright—to ask aright we must ask in the Language of Science
> the only language she can understand—we must first know her
> laws before we can obey them—and we can never know these
> laws except by deep study and constant application.

And again:

> Crops of all kinds have repaid toil, and gratitude is due to the
> beautiful giver from the cultivator of the soil. Let the past year
> retain in its embrace all that is not productive of good, peace and
> happiness, while the new born year takes the sweets of the past
> to invite and encourage onward . . .

To "encourage onward" was another Shaker trait—to urge to improve, to perfect, to excel the world in works which were "useful to man." Brother Philemon Stewart, the head seedsman at the New Lebanon church in the middle of the last century, was constantly experimenting with fruits and berries, developing, among other varieties, the Early Northern Muscadine Grape ("a seedling from the Native White Grape") and The Mountain Seedling Gooseberry of Lebanon, which was discovered growing wild and improved year by year, "both in the quantity and quality of its fruit." In his "Three

Villages," William Dean Howells provides another illustration. Early in August, 1875, the first cultivated blackberries were picked at the Shirley, Mass. community—the new Wachusett berry, a discovery by Brother Leander, "who noticed a vine one day by the wayside on which berries hung ripe, while those on neighboring bushes were yet two weeks from their maturity. He observed also that the cane was almost free from thorns; he marked the vine, and when the leaves fell, transplanted it . . ."

The same characteristic appears in the journals of Alonzo Hollister, the last botanist at New Lebanon, whose association with the herb and extract business covered over a half century, beginning in the late 1850's. Entry after entry records scientific observations and experiments, as when he devotes several finely written pages to the problem of whether water or alcohol constituted the best menstruum, what the proportions of each should be in the case of any given herb, and so on. Author of numerous tracts on the mystical aspects of Shaker theology, this brother exemplified, in his labors, a faith which a leading spokesman of the sect once characterized as "a combination of science, religion and inspiration."

Similar experiments were conducted at Canterbury, where Thomas Corbett gave his name to such once popular products as Corbett's Shaker Syrup of Sarsaparilla, Corbett's Wild Cherry Pectoral Syrup, etc. About 1800 the New Hampshire botanist devised an electro-static machine—probably based on the inventions of Benjamin Franklin (c. 1757)—which, with improvements, was used in the nurse-shops for shocking patients in the treatment of certain nervous disorders.

The blue-wrapped catalogues issued at New Lebanon just prior to the Civil War reveal the scope of the industry at that period. Listed, with prices, are 354 kinds of medicinal plants, barks, roots, seeds and flowers; 156 fluid extracts; 59 solid extracts; 48 "ordinary extracts"; 84 powdered articles; concentrated preparations, including 22 alkaloids and resinoids, 10 ointments, 7 double distilled and fragrant waters and 9 essential oils; and finally, 4 pulverized sweet herbs —sage, thyme, summer savory and sweet marjoram. Particular attention was paid to the drying and grinding of these herbs, to preserve their aroma and strength. They could be either coarsley or finely pulverized—"by the new plan used in the best French Drugmills."

As in the catalogue for 1833, there is a poem on the cover:

A blade of grass—a simple flower,
Cull'd from the dewy lea;
These, these shall speak, with touching power,
Of change and health to thee.

To avoid difficulties in identification the catalogue includes a list of synonyms. Many are old folk names such as Peru apple, bed straw, bees' nest (wild carrot), bouncing-bet (soapwort), chocolate root (Avens's root), Christmas rose (black hellebore), wild coffee (fever root), corn snake root (Button snake root), cure-all (lemon balm), Devil's bit (blazing star), dragon root (wild turnip), dragon's claw (crawley), Eve's cup (side-saddle), fishmouth (snakehead), Gill-go-over-the-ground (ground ivy), goose grass (cleavers), hackmadden (tamarack), healing herb (comfrey), honey bloom (bitter root), itch weed (white hellebore), Jacob's ladder (abscess root), King's clover (mellilot), lamb kill (laurel), leopard bane (arnica), life of man (spikenard), lousewort (betony weed), madweed (scullcap), Moldavian balm (sweet balm), Mohawk weed (bellwort), Monkshood (aconite), mouth root (goldthread), necklace weed and Noah's ark (white cohosh), old man (southernwood), one berry (squaw vine), pipe plant (fit root), pipsissaway (princes pine), polecat weed (skunk cabbage), rattlesnake's master (button snake root), sea thrift (march rosemary), self-heal (heal-all), simplers joy (vervain), smallage (lovage), split rock (alum root), squaw mint (pennyroyal), toothache tree (prickly ash), travellers' joy (Virgin's bower), wake robin (wild turnip), and wild lemon (mandrake).

Though most Shaker herbs were remedial agents it should be noted that besides the four culinary herbs there were other uses. The "fragrant waters," rose water in particular, were sold as perfumes. Lovage root, wild flagroot and horehound were used in confections. Rose water was often used to flavor apple pies. Yellow dock was sold to manufacturers of a well known sarsaparilla. Horse radish had a ready market, as did several kinds of wine, particularly elderberry and currant. Sumac, madder, logwood, golden rod and various barks (butternut, oak, swamp maple, hemlock, chestnut and witch hazel) were sold, or used at home, in the preparation of vegetable dyes.

Closely allied to the herb business, in most of the eighteen societies, was the growing of garden seeds. This industry was even older, originating about 1789 in New Lebanon and Watervliet and somewhat later at Hancock, the two Enfields, and other communities in the east. Culinary vegetables and the proper management of kitchen gardens were basic Shaker interests. The raising of vegetables for seeds also became an exact science, and soon their reputation became as widespread as the herbs. Shaker pedlars in one-horse wagons were a common sight in rural New York and New England. Then, as the business grew, shipments were made to merchants in towns and cities throughout the east, south and west—with a particularly flourishing pre-Civil War trade in the southern states. The center for this trade was the Enfield, Connecticut community, where the business was directed by an enterprising Shaker seedsman, Jefferson White. The broadsides advertising the Enfield products listed, besides vegetable seeds, the following herb-seeds: caraway, coriander, dandelion, dill, fennel, lavender, lemon balm, rosemary, saffron, sage, clary sage, summer savory, sweet basil, sweet marjoram, sweet thyme, marigold pot and rue. Grass seeds were also offered for sale: red clover, white Dutch clover, lucerne or French, blue grass, "herds" (herd's grass) or red top, timothy, millet, canary seed, broom corn seed, Chinese sugar cane, and top or button onion. In its catalogue for 1854 the Enfield society claimed that its seed business, started in 1802, was "the oldest seed establishment in the United States."

In their herb and seed industry the Shakers introduced certain merchandising practices later adopted by the "world." For the wholesale trade they put up seed in cloth bags, but they retailed them in small "papers" or "envelopes" as is the present custom. In 1836 the New Lebanon society also began to issue gardener's manuals, priced at six cents, which gave useful instructions for the selection, preparation and management of a kitchen garden, with additional chapters on injurious insects, the preservation of vegetables in winter, the uses of vegetables, cooking recipes and pickling. Commenting on the right care of a vegetable plot, the compiler notes that "a garden is an index of the owner's mind."

Shaker herbs and garden seeds are associated, in our own minds, not only with the botanists and seedsmen, the manuscripts and manuals

Shakeresses Preparing Herb Extracts

which document the industry and the whole economy of which they were so important a part, but also with the furnishings of the shops where those products were prepared and dispensed. The same fine care was expended on the cupboards, cases of drawers, stands and tables used in the "nurse shops" and "finishing rooms" as on the furniture designed for dwellings and meeting-houses. The small drawers built, row upon row, in one wall of the office occupied by Barnabus Hinckley, the physician at the New Lebanon Church, were neatly dovetailed and finished. Stands for sorting seeds were delicate but sturdy pieces, with rimmed tops. Long, broad-topped tables for packing herbs and roots, the counters on which the sisters packaged the extracts, the label cabinets, baskets and tow sheets used in the industry, all bear the mark of meticulous craftsmanship. Typical infirmary furniture were the two herb cupboards, of butternut wood, used at the North family. Beautifully proportioned, with cupboards above and four deep drawers below, these pieces retain, on the faces of the drawers, such labels as slippery elm, mug wort, hyssop, horehound, sweet fern, liver wort, yarrow, elder flowers, lobelia, summer savory and mallows.

Today, as the Believers themselves are passing away, such artifacts are part of a precious heritage—the call to gardening, herb, seed and kitchen—pursuits practiced not for profit alone, but for service, for the redemption of the soil, for the health of the body and spirit.

"These, these shall speak, with touching power
Of change and health to thee."

Shaker Botanist

IV

THE BRICKYARD

The well-worn road which leads northward from the old Shaker village of New Lebanon cuts into the descending state highway at a sharp angle, forming a corner hazardous to turn by car in slippery weather. Before the concrete highway was laid, the Shaker road continued across and up the mountainside, not sheerly, but at a grade steep enough to make an occasional pause a welcome relief to the pedestrian. Once, too, the grade was a welcome sight for a motorist. For one spring day, as I was driving down Lebanon Mountain, the brakes gave way, and as the car picked up dangerous speed, I chose, on a flash decision, to cut into this by-road. The car spun up the road some twenty or thirty yards, and after losing its momentum backed into a shallow ditch before it came to rest—right side up. That day I thought that Providence itself had made the road, and made it steep!

It was the route followed by the early Believers which led them to their brethren and sisters at the East or Hill family—familiarly called the Brickyard family. Down the road the Shakers drove their ox carts and one-horse wagons with the produce of their acres, or such shopware as chairs, dried sweet corn, brooms and bricks. The road has become all but impassable by car.

When my companion, Bill Winter, the photographer, and I ascended the road by foot one sultry August afternoon, few traces of man's presence remained. From below came the recurrent hum of motors on the highway. To the north, through a line of trees and shrubbery, were glimpses of well-fenced, well-tilled lands, a green valley retreating circuitously westward, and the Catskills in the distance. An occasional chipmunk nibbled kernels from oat straws brushed off the loads by the encroaching woods. Now and then we saw a broken brick, partly concealed in the mucky roadside, evidence of a rural century-old commerce—an inquiry into which was one aim of our climb into the hills. What traces remained of the buildings once occupied by the Brickyard family? Could we find the old dam, or the site of a shop, or the

Elder William Anderson

pit where clay was excavated to be baked and molded into pipe bowls or into the bricks of which many Shaker buildings were made?

Further up, the intervale at our left grew deep and more narrow, forming a gorge which at this season was dry. A path led from the road across what remained of an earthen dam, above which was a swamp of stagnant water. Was it here, we wondered, that Thomas Estes and William Thrasher, and later Elder William Anderson, carried on their trades of making chairs and brooms? Neither a stone nor a timber remained to tell.

But across the road, on our right, were signs of a barn foundation. A few yards further the roadway bent to the right and at this corner we found one objective of our search: a huge slab of stone, and beyond, overgrown with brush and birch saplings, the cellar walls of a dwelling. On a knoll in the midst of this desolation, the granite steps alone remained where the builder had laid them, leading to nothing now but a tangle of weeds and rocks. Beyond was a similar ruin engulfed by the surrounding woods.

A farmer mowing an upland meadow had stopped near us to make some minor repair on his machine. We inquired as to the location of a brickkiln in the area; he was an elderly man, and we thought he might remember. Obligingly—the idea of company in such a lonely place was evidently not displeasing—he guided us through a thicket into a muddy hollow strewn with broken bricks. In one spot there was a mound of them, and here we looked for the great iron kettle, used for boiling corn on the cob, which our guide assured us he once had noticed there. But even that was gone, and the clay pit—"off over thar a bit"—also evaded our search. Our meager stock of knowledge was enlarged, however, by his identification of a second ruin as the kiln in which the famous Shaker green sweet corn was dried.

A brick twice the regulation size and weight was lying by the road, and we found another on the great stone slab which served as the doorstep to the dwelling. These we later lugged down the mountain, shifting them from hand to hand. Simple as these artifacts were, they symbolized, we felt, the philosophy of Shaker industry: Seeking salvation in their own way, the Believers individualized their temporal as well as their spiritual labor, invented tools to solve special problems, and sought to excel the world in all they produced. Bricks were made outsize for particular uses. Even their color seemed to us to be of a softer, purer red than those made in the world.

When it was fully organized early in the last century, under the direction of the New Lebanon Church order, there were two families on the mountain, the East and the West, separated, it appears, by the

Massachusetts-New York state line: the East (Brickyard) was in Hancock, Mass., the West in New Lebanon, N.Y. Once there were two family dwellings, the one at the West a four-story brick structure. At the East family, along with the brickkiln, there was also a laundry, a corn-drying house, a dry kiln and carpenter shop, a two-story broom factory and garden-seed house, a turkey barn, a hen house, a horse barn and a sheep barn accommodating three to four hundred sheep. In the carpentry shop, with lathes and planing machines run by water power, some of the earliest Shaker chairs were made.

Many tales could be told of strange happenings in these old Shaker families. Not long ago we met a Hancock farmer, aged 84, whose father had worked for many years at the Brickyard. One of the stories handed down to him concerned the ritual of "burying the devil," a rite his father claimed he had witnessed. It seems that the devil—"Old Ugly" as the Shakers called him—was seen lurking about the premises, the alarm was raised, and after a frantic chase he was finally cornered, seized and buried in a pit. The pit was then covered with earth, and heavy stones piled on to so the devil could not escape.

Another story concerned an old man who called at the Shaker dwelling one cold Christmas day, with the temperature 35 degrees below zero. He came, he said, because he wanted to talk with God, and asked if he could go into the "East room" and be left alone. The request was granted, and for an hour or more he could be heard talking and praying. "You don't know how much good this has done me," he confided after he came out. The Shakers wanted him to stay, warning him that he would freeze to death if he continued his journey. But he had accomplished what he came to do, he said, in the place he had chosen, and with no further word he walked away into the dark and cold.

Our Hancock informant was a great admirer of Shaker furniture. Gazing at a rocking chair in the room where we were talking, he said, "What more do you want for beauty. . . . When they made anything, they *made* it."

The Brickyard family was dissolved nearly a century ago. Death claimed all of its members, and wilderness reclaimed the land. Only one do we remember, the aforementioned William Anderson, whom we once saw resting in the sun on the steps of the South Family dwelling. The patriarch was bent over, leaning on his cane, his long white beard reaching nearly to the ground. We saw him only once. He seemed incredibly old.

V

THE LORD'S STONE AND TWO CROSSES

In a drawer of a blue built-in cupboard in the old Hancock meeting house we once found a collection of manuscript books which documented, in great detail, the strange meetings held during the so-called "Era of the Manifestations," from 1837 onward for more than ten years. Among them were eyewitness accounts taken down by appointed scribes of the mountain "love feasts" which were celebrated twice a year, in May and September, in all the Shaker communities.

The few remaining Believers are reticent about these meetings, as well as those held in their churches during the three year period (1842-45) when the world was excluded from their Sabbathday services. David Lamson, an apostate from the Hancock society, wrote about them in a little book published in 1848, and there are fragmentary accounts from other sources. But the Shakers themselves sought to keep them secret.

We had read in Lamson about the marble tablets, engraved with "The Word of the Lord for the Healing of the Nations," which were placed at one end of the hexagonal fenced enclosures called "fountains." We knew that the feast grounds were located on secluded hilltops within each community's domain. We had also heard that at New Lebanon two wooden crosses were erected, one in front of the meeting house and the other in front of the trustees' office, warning the public away. These were historical facts. We knew that the stones, the sites, the crosses, the meetings once actually existed, but they had become unreal, even legendary. The Shakers themselves had almost forgotten about them. The wilderness had reclaimed the clearings where the meetings were held. The Lord's stones had either been secretly buried, or broken up by vandals. The crosses, too, had disappeared. Gone, apparently forever, was all tangible evidence of Mother Ann's mysterious "work"—her "Second Appearing"—in this period.

The discovery of the Hancock records, hidden away in an obscure cupboard, was therefore an exciting experience, the first of three which made the manifestations real. There were some eight or ten bound

Shown here and on opposite page are fragments of the Lord's Stone from Tyringham, Massachusetts.

books, carefully written, recording the spiritual messages or communications received by the leaders of the society and describing the feast days and Christmas meetings at Hancock (The City of Peace), Enfield, Connecticut (The City of Union) and Tyringham (The City of Love). If the ministry, concerned lest the world ridicule these strange rites, had ordered these records destroyed, the injunction had never been carried out. We could visualize the sisters, whose function it was to serve as scribes, depositing their work in "the most holy sanctuary," reluctant to destroy what had been recorded with such faith and care.

The second experience took place in the little village of Tyringham. Overlooking a deep-walled valley, a few sturdy buildings, known as "Fernside" on Jerusalem Road, survive to tell us of one of the loveliest of Shaker colonies. Higher up the mountain were the feast grounds, which the Shakers had named Mount Horeb. Seeking to learn more about Horeb, we chanced one day on a villager who recalled that pieces

of a sacred stone, which he had heard had something to do with Shaker worship, were still preserved in the town library. This little building was open only a few hours in the week, but we managed to find the librarian, who graciously let us in. And there, on a broad window sill, were the fragments of marble, parts of the tablet which had been written and placed on the mountain top over a century ago "by the command of our Lord and Saviour Jesus Christ." These literal symbols of mystic rites— what emotions they stirred! For the first time we were acutely aware that the Lord's command had indeed been obeyed, that Mother Ann's children, arrayed in their colorful spiritual garments actually did march twice a year to this holy ground and around a "fountain" danced and sang, sowed spiritual seed and reaped the harvest, ate spiritual food, welcomed Indian spirits into their midst, exchanged spiritual gifts, and offered on an altar of stones their choicest possessions: humility, simplicity, union, peace and love. Here was an artifact—"broken by

FRUITS OF THE SHAKER TREE OF LIFE

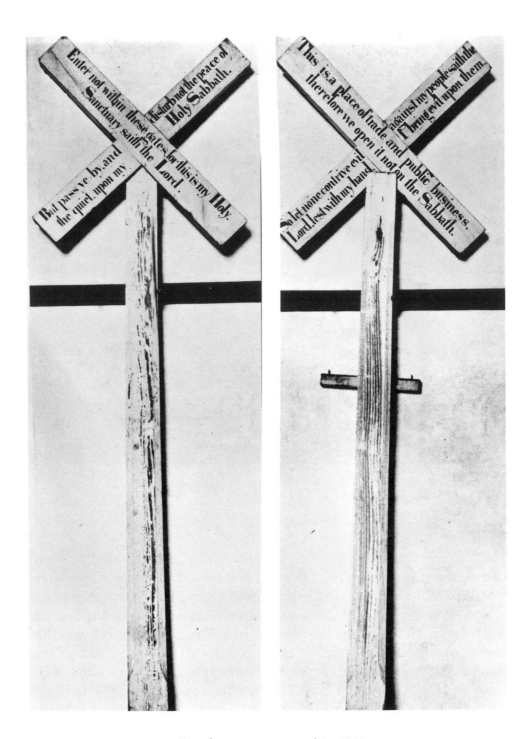

Wooden crosses erected in 1842

some of the wicked" in June, 1851—that turned legend into fact. Our feelings were akin to those who discovered the Dead Sea scrolls, or the lunar ship of the night of the great pharaoh Cheops.

The wooden crosses were the third unexpected find. We had read that the revelations which came to the Shakers in the early 1840's were of such a startling nature that the resultant rituals transcended all traditional forms. The dances became more ecstatic, more promiscuous than ever before. Visions and visitations of departed spirits abounded. Prophecies, trances, "bodily operations," exercises of all kinds were so phenomenal that the ministry decided, in 1842, to close the meetings to a public which had ordinarily been welcome to the Sabbath services. We had read that crosses had been erected at New Lebanon with a proclamation warning the world away, but supposed that these had long since been destroyed.

It came as a surprise, then, to find, stacked away in a corner of the top loft of the barrel-roofed meeting house, another proof that these fantastic rituals had once been observed. When the public meetings were reopened in 1845 the crosses, set on top of long posts, had been stored to await, perhaps, another awakening that never occurred. But there they were, bearing mute testimony that a great wave of spiritual fervor, half a century or more after Mother Ann's death, had again flooded the community with its cleansing power.

On one cross were the printed words:

> Enter not within these gates, for this is my Holy
> Sanctuary saith the Lord
> But pass ye by, and disturb not the peace of
> the quiet, upon my Holy Sabbath.

The other bore the following legend:

> This is a place of trade and public business,
> therefore we open it not on the Sabbath
> So let none contrive evil against my people, saith the
> Lord, lest with my hand, I bring evil upon them.

The crosses were first put up on May 1, 1842, and the public meetings closed. In the official "Records of the Church" at New Lebanon for that date is this interesting note:

> And early in the morning, on the first of May, there were found on
> the fence three papers . . . . having this scripture on them:
> 'Neither do men light a candle, and put it under a bushel. Let your
> light shine, etc.'

Nevertheless, for three years the Shaker light ceased to shine on the world, though within the community it glowed with new intensity.

We photographed the crosses. But some years later, when the Shaker property had changed hands, we looked in vain for them. In vain until one day, in the course of planning a project on Shaker architecture, we had occasion to make a survey of the brethren's brick shop at the Church family, a building long disused. In the cellar there was a mass of miscellaneous discarded material—stair rails, window frames, broken down cupboards and drawers, baskets, coopersware, machine and shop tools—a tangled mass, a mess. But in the half-light two lines of white caught our attention, revealing themselves on closer inspection, as the upright and cross piece of one of the crosses. There it lay in the midst of clutter, but with its message bravely surviving the hand of indifferent men.

As we write these notes in the spring of 1963 we can report, with gratitude, that the crosses were finally rescued from oblivion, and now are installed in the restored Shirley, Massachusetts, Shaker meeting house moved to Hancock. They bear testimony to one of the strangest chapters in the history of religion in America.

VI

THE WHILOM HOUSE *

SHAKER ORDERS CONCERNING THE DEAD

At the North family in New Lebanon, New York, there is a two-story frame shop once used by the Shaker pattern makers, coopers and carpenters. Many tools of the trade were still lying around on benches and in cupboards when, in the middle 1920's, we first started our collecting. We would open doors and peer into cupboards, never knowing what object would meet the eye.

One day, in exploring the shop, we happened on a storeroom whose door was closed but unlocked. Investigation disclosed that it was the room for keeping homemade coffins used by the Believers till late in the last century. Three or four were piled up on one side of the room—unvarnished, plain, but cleanly made of native white pine and neatly dovetailed.

A coffin is a coffin, evoking sad thoughts of mortality. But these pieces were also examples of fine Shaker craftsmanship, and as the society was now using worldly caskets, we asked if we could acquire one. We already possessed two of the hickory and ash racks on which the coffin was carried to the grave, some of the white woven sashes with which it was bound to the rack and lowered into the ground, and examples of the early Shaker pleated shrouds of white glazed cambric with a narrow belt. But alas, it was decreed that furniture for the dead was not to go out into the world. And on a subsequent visit to the shop the coffins had disappeared.

The episode reminded us of a poem in "Shaker Burials" written in 1877 for *The Shaker,* the monthly periodical of the society, published, under different titles from 1871 to 1899. The author was Louis Basting, for many years an elder at the Hancock Church family. Brother Louis was not ordinarily given to poetic expression, though he wrote a few pamphlets on doctrine. The present piece, parts of which we quote, has interest not only for the viewpoint it gives on the topic, but as an

* Reprinted by permission of *New-England Galaxy,* Sturbridge, Massachusetts. Edward Deming Andrews, "The Whilom House, Shaker Orders Concerning the Dead," *New-England Galaxy,* Fall 1965, Vol. VIII, No. 2, p. 46.

example of the dry wit which frequently cropped out in the utterances of a supposedly humorless people. Basting begins:

> There is just now much agitation,
> Much study and deep cogitation
> Upon the subject of cremation. . . .

Of widespread concern is this "business" of the dead,

> For soon or late all will be tested
> By some *post mortem* operation
> Regardless of their inclination. . . .
> And since (man) loved his body well,
> He takes good care of the old shell—
> He thinks 'twill resurrected be
> When Gabriel sounds the reveille.
> Meantime he seeks the grave's repose,
> There quietly to decompose. . . .

After references to the burial customs of the Egyptians, Parsees, Romans, Moslems and American Indians, the poet passes to the present:

> Folly seems to bear the sway
> In rosewood coffin, silver-plated,
> Velvet-lined and satin-braided;
> On flashy hearse, 'neath waving plume,
> They bear the dead man to his tomb;
> And by the length of the procession,
> Men judge the worth of his profession. . . .

In contrast:

> The Shakers, hating vain display,
> When their beloved ones pass away.
> Make short and simple preparation,
> Void of all worldly ostentation,
> In simple robes, but without stain,
> In coffin neat, unvarnished, plain,
> They bear the whilom house away,
> Wherein the spirit used to stay;
> And singing a sweet song or two,
> They bid their friends farewell, adieu.
> The traffic of the undertakers
> Would not pay well among the Shakers.

Brother Louis ends his poem by returning to the subject of cremation:

> Carbon is of the greatest need,
> Without its aid, we should, indeed,
> Cease to exist and pass away,
> Like mist before the solar ray.

But when man's mission on this earth is done, "the imprisoned carbon" in the physical organism is set free. "To be wasted, or used again?" the poet asks, concluding that "we needs must have the body burn." He continues:

> But when we burn with fire, the gas
> Goes upward into air, whereas
> When taking place below the ground,
> In nutriment it will abound.

So the Shakers buried their dead, marking the spot with a simple stone engraved only with the initials (and later the name) of the deceased, the age, and the date of death. They even considered abandoning this custom, substituting, as a more fitting memorial, a shrub, vine or fruit tree to perpetuate the usefulness of the departed.

"Orders concerning the dead" were given in the Millennial Laws of the Shakers, as revised in 1845. They read in part:

> [1.] When the spirit is departing and a person is breathing the last, all present should kneel in prayer.
> 2. In an hour after the breath has left the body, the corpse may be laid out in the fear of God.
> 3. A corpse should be dressed in a shirt and winding sheet, a handkerchief, and a muffler if necessary,—and for a female, add thereto a cap and collar.
> 4. The laying out, dressing and burial of a corpse is the duty of the Deacons and Deaconesses to direct. . . .
> 5. Children under twelve years of age, are not allowed to attend any funerals, save in the family where they live. . . .

Two more orders are included in "The Holy Orders of the Church" (1841), an earlier version of the Laws:

> Ye shall not bring up the faults and failings of the dead, to talk and converse upon. For this is displeasing to departed spirits, to your Heavenly Parents, and to God, your Heavenly Father.
> Always be still, and keep the fear of God, when there is a corpse in the family, for the Heavenly Hosts, is then near you.

The Shaker attitude towards death was summed up, seventy-five years ago, by three elders of the North family at New Lebanon: Daniel Fraser, Frederick Evans, and Richard Bushnell. When a visitor to the settlement asked Elder Daniel to see the graveyard, his reply was that there was little there of interest. "The graves are barely marked," he said, and for his part he would "as lief be buried without a mortuary token" at his head. "Of what use were a few handfuls of dust, and what honor need attend them? The life and deeds of a man were not interred."

At the funeral of Brother John Greves of the North family on 12 September, 1886, the subject was discussed at length in Elder Frederick's sermon, "He is not here." After reminding the company that the Shakers did not believe in the future reanimation of the body, he compared the "human error and folly" of the Egyptians and other peoples, ancient and modern (of embalming the body as a means of preserving its identity) with the experience of Martha and Mary at the sepulchre of Jesus. "True to the Egyptian instinct still latent in them, (they) had come in the morning, bringing sweet spices with which to embalm the dead body. But they met a vision of angels, who said, 'He is risen. He is not here.' "

Even "the idea of keeping in mind, from generation to generation, the spot where the body was deposited" was, in the elder's mind, preposterous, because the body decomposes and becomes "mingled with the general elements." Even the body, then, is not here; it has gone into "the community of earth."

The elder's prescription was to, "Build a good decent fence and gather up all the stones, form a paper plot; level the ground, or round up the graves, plant a timber tree by each grave and calmly await the consequences."

Elder Richard, like his predecessor, called attention to "the absurdity of the long taught doctrine of the resurrection of the material," which he felt was being "fast exploded." On the other hand, believing that there should be "a proper degree of respect due to the body, after the man or woman is elsewhere," he proposed that Shaker burying grounds should be attractive spots, neatly fenced and cared for. "I would begin at one end, and bury along its side in a straight row. . . . As the graves settle, they would, for a time require to be handsomely rounded up. . . . Of course a record of the burial should be kept. . . ."

These are quotations from a small booklet (15pp.), entitled "Shaker Sermon" (1886), by Elder F. W. Evans. The booklet concludes with a brief article on funeral reform, "a new enterprise" by the Church of England Funeral and Mourning Association, which deprecated "the spending of large sums, undoubtedly from a natural and laudable desire to pay honor to the departed, on an ostentatious funeral and mourning." The Association advocated economy and simplicity: the use of plain hearses, the disuse of crape, etc., the avoidance of excessive floral decoration, meeting in the church or cemetery instead of the house of mourning, disuse of club money on funerals, early interment, and the use of such materials for the coffin as will rapidly decay after burial (for reasons of health).

It was our privilege to be present at two Shaker funerals. At one in 1935, that of our dear friend Sister Alice, I was chosen as a pallbearer. I will never forget the experience of bearing the casket, in the company of three Shaker brethren, from the dwelling up the snow-laden slope to the grave under the brow of Mt. Sinai, the holy mountain of the Hancock community. It was bitter cold. Without ceremony we lowered the coffin into the ground on the wind-swept hillside. Our final tribute was silence.

The other funeral was that of Elder Walter of the North family at New Lebanon. Three brethren sat stiffly on a bench in the meeting room in front of the coffin: Brother Benny of the Church family, who seemed distracted and uneasy; Hamilton of the Watervliet society, a long-faced, square-jawed, usually garrulous brother; and white-bearded Ricardo of Hancock, who resembled, an immobile Roman statue. Outwardly the most affected was the hired man Carl—a tall, emaciated figure dressed in a faded black frock coat—who stood alone in a corner of the room, expressionless but conscious surely of an ir-reparable loss, a bond broken, the passing of one who had given him, a poor laborer from the world, kindness and understanding. As the hymns were sung, Carl bowed his head and tears rolled down his face. Other laborers on the farm, selected as pallbearers, gathered in a group by the door, phlegmatic and ill-at-ease.

Opposite the brethren sat the Shaker sisters, seven or eight in all, dressed, with one exception, in their Sabbathday gray, homespun garments. Some wore white wool shawls. The exception was Martha, an elderly sister in the family, an individualist with outspoken con-victions on many subjects. Martha came in a wine-colored dress.

Following traditional Shaker ritual, the service was a simple but impressive one consisting of hymns and tributes by any who cared to speak, with periods of silence between. The presiding elder, Arthur Bruce of the Canterbury society, reminded us that "we are living now, that we always live, in the midst of eternity." After his few earnest words Sister Rosetta, calm and controlled, her face illumined with a spiritual light, read the twenty-third psalm. And when, at the end of the service, the coffin was borne through the doorway on its way to the burying ground in a nearby grove, it was Rosetta who led the Shaker funeral hymn, "Bear me away," waving her hands gently in a rhythmic, moving farewell to him who had been her "elder brother."

In the early years of the order it was said that the spirit of the de-parted was often present at the service, testifying, through a medium or "instrument," to the happiness of eternal life.

VII

THE HISTORICAL ANN LEE

It was some time before we thought of Ann Lee, the foundress of the Shaker sect, as a person who actually lived, spoke and suffered as a mortal in this world. She had remained a shadowy figure whose name appeared in old manuscripts and books, a personage so obscured by legend and the strange powers attributed to her that she was more a symbol of Shaker beliefs than a woman of flesh and blood. Despite all the documents recording her work and travail, she herself, being illiterate, left no writing as evidence of her thought and experience. She remained remote in time, and time had even erased almost all traces of the places she knew in England. When we visited Toad Lane in Manchester, where she was born and spent her childhood, we found Toad Lane changed to Todd Street, and so changed in character that it was difficult to realize it had once been the place of squalid shops and dwellings that Ann had known. Only the cathedral from which she had been ejected for "disturbing the congregation" remained as a landmark of her era.

Banns of Marriage, Abraham Standerin and Ann Lees

Three experiences served to diminish this curious sense of unreality about the prophetess. Seeking to obtain some record of Mother Ann's early life, and particularly of her fateful marriage to the blacksmith, Abraham Stanley (or Standerin), we wrote to the John Rylands library in Manchester. There was nothing there, but a helpful official of the library offered to search the records of the cathedral for the banns of the marriage. The search was successful, and in due time a photostat of the document, with the crosses by which the principals had signed their names, was sent to us. Just two small crooked lines crossing, but they had been made by Ann's own hand, and in the act and its transmittal down the years, she became a real person.

The second experience occurred several years later on the occasion of a visit we were making to Niskeyuna, the community at Watervliet, N.Y. where Mother Ann and her little band of religious pioneers made their first home in America. Over the years we had come to know and love Anna Case, the last presiding eldress of that colony which was soon to be closed forever. Here it was that, for the first time, we became "partakers with the Shakers" in a meal where no word was spoken. Here, in an abandoned sisters' shop, we found one of our choicest pieces of furniture, a curly maple counter, stained red, with small ebony colored drawer pulls (now in the American Museum in Britain). But what revitalized the foundress was a gift, presented without ostentation by Eldress Anna: a piece of Mother Ann's dress. No likeness of Mother Ann exists. Even the descriptions of her appearance vary. Yet through this association item—a bit of cloth with sober-colored stripes—one came into her physical presence.

Most moving of all was the pilgrimage we made, one sunny morning in early May 1937, to the Shaker burying ground at Watervliet. We had driven through the congestion of Albany and the housing developments of its outskirts. Planes occasionally broke the silence over the airport which once was Shaker land. We had been depressed by the slum-like appearance of the buildings and yards of what were formerly the neat, orderly South and West families. Then we came to the peaceful enclosure, shaded by old trees, where the Niskeyuna Believers are laid to rest.

The stones, plain rectangular slabs of granite, were all alike—all but the one which marked the grave of Mother Ann, it was a little higher and included, besides the name, age and date of death (Sept. 8, 1784, aged 48, 6, 8), her place of birth, Manchester, England. On either side of this central stone were the markers commemorating, oh so simply, five of her staunchest followers: closest to her, her own brother, Father William Lee, and her successor "in the female line," Mother Lucy Wright; then Elder John Hocknell, whose munificence made possible the hegira to America, Eldress Ruth Landon, appointed by Mother Lucy to be "first among the sisters" in the central ministry, and Elder Abiathar Babbitt, who succeeded Father Joseph Meacham in the male leadership of the order.

The circumstances of Ann's death are as shrouded in mystery as the early years of her life. She died one year after the conclusion of an arduous mission through parts of New York and New England, a journey marked by constant hardship, persecution and at times physical mistreatment. Was her death a natural one? One wonders. For when the remains were disinterred for removal to the Shaker cemetery, there was evidence that her skull had been fractured and that she may therefore have died from wounds suffered on that mission. There may be corroboration in the fact that in the eventful year following her successful tour, no record exists of her part in what by that time was a burgeoning movement.

VIII

A PEWTER PLATE AND
FOUR STANDS

It was a chilly day late in March. Snow lay around the Ann Lee cottage to which the Neale sisters, Emma and Sadie, had moved from the Church family office. While Faith was talking with Sister Sadie in her shop, I was wandering aimlessly about outside. By the back door, on a small patch of ground bared by the spring sunshine, a dish of food had been set out for the family cat. (It should here be explained that, according to the *Millennial Laws,* cats could be kept in shops with permission, but "no dogs in any family gathered into order.")

A casual glance seemed to indicate that the dish was a cheap tin plate. I passed on. Then the thought struck me: tin plates do not have a narrow molded rim, but usually flare out flatly. Returning for a closer look, I discovered it was pewter. Sadie wondered why we should want a cat dish, but said we could have it.

When we reached home and had the plate well-scoured, the maker's name was revealed: Danforth, with the eagle touch used by William (1769-1820). Measuring six inches in diameter, it belonged in the category of "rare" and from then on occupied a special place on a hanging rack in our living room.

Except for pewter buttons and the molds used in making pipe bowls, the Shakers did not work in the metal. Pewter dishes, however, were often used in the early days, purchased from the world or brought in by converts. The Danforth plate, with other pieces found in the communities, encouraged us to collect this ware, and we now have a representative collection of pewter used by the Shakers.

The pewter dish was only one of many unexpected finds. At New Lebanon there were a number of unused shops which we were permitted to explore to our heart's desire. Among them was the early meeting-house, a building which had been converted into a three-story garden seed house after the second church, a much larger one,

Early stands from the New Lebanon Church family. Ferdinand's stand, a transition piece, is at far right; stick-leg extension reading stand is second from right.

Sister Lillian Barlow

An early cherry lightstand from the Second family. Now in the American Museum in Britain.

was built in 1822-24. Many rooms were empty. In others were seed bins, barrels, boxes and the miscellaneous clutter of an abandoned industry.

One hot July day we were roaming through this spacious shop, occasionally finding a tool, a packet of labels or some other article to add to our industrial collection. In an upper room stood several barrels of corn cobs, from one of which projected three sticks or rods. Curious to know what they were attached to, we tried to extract whatever it was from the cobs only to find that it resisted all our tugging. So we dug out the cobs with our hands until we finally uncovered, to our surprise and delight, a very early peg-leg stand, with a rim top and neat little drawer, all in perfect condition!

The subject of stands brings to mind another adventure, one in which patience rather than accident played the leading role.

Brother Ferdinand was one of the last male members of the Church family at New Lebanon. His retiring room was in the basement of a large brick dwelling, a well-lighted room looking out over an orchard and hills to the south. When we knew him he was well along in years, infirm and long past productive labor. Most of his time was spent in this room, though we sometimes came across him taking a short walk, moving slowly along with the aid of a Shaker cane.

One day we paid him a visit. What we talked about is now forgotten, but the memory of our first sight of the stand beside his bed is still distinct. It was the only piece of Shaker-made furniture in the room. There was nothing on the stand, no book, no pipe, no glass of water. It seemed to have no use.

However, on inquiring further if it could be purchased, we were informed that it was "Ferdinand's stand," that it was his favorite piece and that it *did* have a use—he placed his watch on it at night! And to make sure it remained at his bedside one foot was screwed to the floor.

That was that. It did no good to suggest that another stand, a new one perhaps, be substituted for the one we coveted. Ferdinand would sorely miss the one he had used for over fifty years. We would have to wait.

After some seven or eight years Brother Ferdinand no longer had need to put his watch on the stand at night. And when he was no longer in time, the sisters kept their promise to let us have what time had withheld so long.

It was never easy to buy furniture, or anything else, from the Second family at New Lebanon. In our time there were only two covenant members left in the family. One had retired to his room, where he slept, read and had his meals. He was seldom seen. The other, Sister Lillian Barlow, was busy with cooking, canning, gardening, or sewing (she was an accomplished seamstress), but devoted most of her time to making chairs in a barn-like building near the family dwelling. One was almost sure to find her somewhere in the large noisy chair room cluttered with lathes, sanding machines, steam racks and all the accouterments of the industry. Though only one machine might be in use, generally several were operating, the worn leather belts flapping and whirling as they revolved on the pulleys of the overhead shafts. Somewhere in the room was her co-worker, William Perkins, a heavyset, mustached Englishman with a knowledge of mechanics, who had come into the family years before and stayed on.

They were always cordial, but the work never stopped and one had to shout to be heard above the din of the belts and wheels, and the chisels biting into the maple chair posts. There was seldom time to sit down and talk, to say nothing of searching under their guidance for the treasures we knew lay neglected in the many rooms of the dwelling. The cellars were large, cool caverns filled with everything imaginable, the cast-off household equipment of a century and a quarter—old tables, glass, pewter, domestic utensils of all kinds. Most of the rooms were locked.

Besides, Lillian was loath to part with anything except the chairs she was making, these and her flowers, or her asparagus, or sometimes old books and manuscripts. She had a strong sentimental attachment to any piece of Shaker workmanship—to sell it was to part with a part of her past; to admit, perhaps, that there was no future for one of the oldest New Lebanon families.

Nevertheless we did obtain, or more properly speaking, successfully beg several pieces from this loyal Shakeress—pieces which we were proud to own, as the Second family numbered among its members some of the best craftsmen in the society. Two of the finest items in our whole collection came from this source: a pair of cherry lightstands—light in weight as in function—which we have always felt are perfect examples of Shaker design. The tops are round and thin, the slim posts subtly taper, the umbrella feet are simple arcs. Delicately proportioned and refined in line, they are studies in pure geometric form, symbols of the highest ideals of the Shaker faith.

When we started collecting—early Americana as well as Shaker—we occasionally attended country auctions, sometimes bringing along the playpen in an effort to confine our young son. Rarely did we acquire anything of note; someone always outbid us. But the auctions were great fun and often an educational experience.

At one vendue, however, held at a country estate near the New Lebanon community, we learned that among "the articles too numerous to mention" was an unusual stick-leg extension reading stand which sounded Shaker, and when we came to the preview, found to *be* Shaker. It was an early piece, stained a soft pink, in original condition. We could visualize a tall Shaker elder or the "public preacher" —perhaps Frederick W. Evans himself—standing before it as he read from the scriptures or *The Testimony of Christ's Second Appearing.* How we wanted it! And how determined we were to get it!

The day came. There were crowds there. Waiting for the cherished piece to be put up we mingled with the people, impatient and anxious. And when it was time, we found ourselves in different parts of the yard.

Someone started bidding, at five and then ten dollars. Others joined in. The bids went up to twenty, twenty-five, thirty dollars. I was getting panicky. Faith usually took the initiative on such occasions, but I couldn't see her, or hear her—naturally, as her method was to signal to the auctioneer with a nod, or with a shake of the head. When the bidding had gone to fifty, most of the bidders dropped out. But one does not lose a prize for a few dollars, so I joined in with sixty dollars. A solitary competitor bid sixty-five. I raised it to seventy. The other person went up another five, and then what happened? Each bidder now being curious to know his or her opponent, there was recognition at last. My competitor was my wife!

IX

THE SCHOOLHOUSE ATTIC

What would one expect to find in the attic of a Shaker school-house which had been closed for over thirty years? Certainly we didn't know.

It was a trim little structure set against the hillside, with a stone foundation which served as the western wall of the first story. Many a time we had peered through the basement windows, making mental note of an old book cupboard with glass doors, which was barely visible along a further wall. Little, we suspected, had been moved out since the house was raised in 1839. So when we were finally given the key and permission to explore, all the pleasure of anticipation was ours.

Opening the front door we entered the shadowy basement room, finding there not one but two old cupboards. Narrow stairs led to the main schoolroom, well lighted by windows on three sides. Adjoining it was a small anteroom, probably a teacher's study, from which another flight of stairs led to the attic.

The schoolroom was a disappointment. It was furnished with the usual equipment: desks bought from some supply house, maps, apparatus used in teaching science, and so on. Nothing of interest except an old Columbia County, New York, map and an Audubon bird chart; nothing Shaker except a homemade clock-like device for teaching pupils how to read the time of day. Textbooks lay strewn about on the teacher's table, the desks, the floor. Except for the white peg-lined walls it could have been any country schoolroom in New York state.

Then, as we climbed the attic stairs, time turned back a century. For here were stored the desks and benches which the Shakers made soon after schools were first organized in the Children's Order, back in 1817. The Lancasterian, or monitor method of teaching, was then becoming popular, and these fine old pine desks, accommodating six pupils each, three on each side, answered the purposes of group in-

Shaker School at Mount Lebanon

struction. Two of these interesting pieces, with a number of later desks at which four pupils sat in a single row, stood in a veritable sea of books and pamphlets, pads, papers and ink bottles. Apparently at some time everything on the second story had been moved into the attic and the school had been modernized with equipment from the world.

Old pamphlets are fascinating for one never knows what will turn up. Here on the attic floor, among the books and papers, were hundreds of them, dusty, rumpled, forgotten. We had visions of rare finds, copies perhaps of the famous Rathbun, West or Taylor tracts, published in the 1730's, or Father Joseph Meacham's "True Principles," with its Bennington, Vt., 1790 title page. Anything could show up in this mass of imprints.

Here in the dark, hot chamber under the roof was a research project which required perseverance. Ever hopeful, we pursued it systematically, starting in at one end of the low room, crawling along on hands and knees, peering at titles, laying aside anything at all interesting. The Rathbuns didn't show up. Neither did Benjamin West, nor Amos Taylor. Why, after all, would the Shakers preserve docu-

An early Shaker schoolroom with desk, bench and hanging bookrack. The "clock" device on the wall is from the Watervliet settlement. It is dated 1870.

ments in which they had been attacked so bitterly? We found a few books and pamphlets published by the Believers themselves, desirable items but already represented in our library by several copies.

Then we came upon a nest of oblong booklets bound in the blue paper with yellow-dusted edges and strips of wine-colored tape on the spines. A glance at the title page showed they had been printed, in clear bold type, on a hand press. The reading proved it was Shaker: *A Short Abridgement of the Rules of Music With Lessons For Exercise, and A few Observations; For new Beginners,* by Isaac N. Youngs, printed at New Lebanon, 1843.

The pamphlet had been listed in J.P. MacLean's bibliography, but up to now we had not been able to locate a single copy. Here were twenty or more: some were the first edition, and the others, the reprint of 1846. Obviously, soon after the school house was built, this was the manual which the singing teachers, including Youngs himself, had used to instruct their charges in the peculiar musical notation developed by the Shakers. Here, also, was added evidence of native genius: for Isaac was already known to us as a clockmaker, reelwright, tailor, blacksmith, mason, farmer, and historian.

Descending the stairs, we were stiff, grimy, and sweaty, but exceedingly happy. We were sure we could obtain the cupboards, the desks and benches. And the finding of the "Rules"—which eventually opened up a whole new field of research—was like discovering a new land.

X

BARN YIELDS

Not often does a barn yield much of value to the collector except tools and the usual paraphernalia to be found on a farm. Sometimes, if one is lucky, he may come across a bench or stool or maybe a table that is not beyond restoration. Two of the best X-trestle tables we ever had came from barns: one, a short sawbuck made of chestnut, from a dilapidated barn in Stephentown, N.Y.; the other, from the cellar of a Shaker barn, a ten-foot beauty with a hole in one end for grading apples. Mention has already been made of the twenty-foot trestle table from a Shaker mill. It is not wise to pass up any old building, house, shed, or barn.

Once, we were wandering through the outbuildings at the Sabbathday Lake (Maine) community, we saw tacked on a stable wall an old chart in watercolor of the Alfred (Maine) Shaker village, and near it, lying on the beam, a scroll tied up with string. The brother who was our guide knew that the scroll was made up of other paintings, but they had been left where the artists had consigned them years ago. All were ours for the asking.

The Alfred chart was a representation of the Church, Second, and North families. We found that the scroll contained plans of three other communities: Poland Hill, New Gloucester (both in Maine) and Canterbury, New Hampshire. Two were dated Jan. 1, 1850 and signed by one Joshua H. Bussell. All four were done with care in detail and charm in color. There was pride, obviously, in the accomplishment.

Why then were they left in a barn and not framed to adorn the wall of some family dwelling? The following passage from the *Millennial Laws,* which were the guide to "temporal order," supplies the answer:

> No maps, Charts, and no pictures or paintings, shall ever be hung in your dwelling-rooms, shops, or Office. And no pictures or paintings set in frames, with glass before them shall ever be among you.

THE

TESTIMONY

OF

CHRIST's SECOND APPEARING;

CONTAINING

A GENERAL STATEMENT

OF

ALL THINGS PERTAINING TO THE FAITH AND
PRACTICE OF THE CHURCH OF GOD
IN THIS LATTER-DAY.

———

PUBLISHED BY ORDER OF THE MINISTRY,
IN UNION WITH THE CHURCH.

Now is come salvation, and strength, and the kingdom of our
God, and the power of his Christ.   REVELATION..

SECOND EDITION, CORRECTED AND IMPROVED..

ALBANY :

PRINTED BY E. AND E. HOSFORD.....STATE-STREET.

———

1810.

Title page from the book found in an upper loft at the Hancock Community.

FOURTH EDITION.
SHAKERS.

COMPENDIUM

OF THE

ORIGIN, HISTORY, PRINCIPLES, RULES AND REGULATIONS,
GOVERNMENT, AND DOCTRINES

OF THE

UNITED SOCIETY OF BELIEVERS IN CHRIST'S
SECOND APPEARING.

WITH BIOGRAPHIES OF
ANN LEE,

WILLIAM LEE, JAS. WHITTAKER, J. HOCKNELL, J. MEACHAM,
AND LUCY WRIGHT.

BY F. W. EVANS.

O my soul, swallow down understanding, and devour wisdom;
for thou hast only time to live."—ESDRAS.

NEW LEBANON, N.Y

1867.

An undistributed pamphlet by Elder F.W. Evans

In the Shaker mind a picture was a "superfluity," a useless ornament.

Literary finds were no less exciting. For there is something about the discovery of a book, pamphlet or manuscript to add to one's library that is as rewarding as finding a chair or table of variant design. Elsewhere we have told of the thrill which came from rummaging in the schoolhouse at New Lebanon. In the upper loft, or attic, of the brick dwelling at Hancock we once found ten mint copies of the Albany, 1810, edition of *The Testimony of Christ's Second Appearing,* the second printing of the book sometimes called the Shaker "bible." In the same community, tucked away in the corner of the cupboard, we chanced on a copy of the *Testimonies of the Life, Character, Revelations and Doctrines of Our Ever Blessed Mother Ann Lee,* the so-called "secret book of the elders," printed at Hancock in 1816, of which only three other copies are known. On another occasion, among some papers in a blanket chest, we found what is our earliest manuscript, the prophetic letter, dated Ashfield, Mass. 1787, which Father James Whittaker, Mother Ann's successor, had written to Josiah Talcott, a farmer in Hancock, urging him to improve his lands in anticipation of the Shaker colony which was destined to be founded there. Ledgers, day-books, diaries, journals, letters, hymnals, indentures, discharges, recipes, manifestoes—these were turning up everywhere—in dwellings, offices, or ministry shops.

But on a rainy day in spring, as we were looking through an almost empty barn at the Second family in New Lebanon, we noticed an unopened packing box—no label on it, no marks of any kind. Receiving permission to open it, we found it contained the entire edition (the fourth) of a Shaker pamphlet entitled: *Compendium of the Origin, History, Principles, Rules and Regulations, Government, and Doctrines of the United Society of Believers in Christ's Second Appearing. With Biographies of Ann Lee, William Lee, Jas. Whittaker, J. Hocknell, J. Meacham, and Lucy Wright.* (New Lebanon, N.Y., 1867.)

The author was F.W. Evans, the North family elder often considered the chief spokesman of the sect. For some unknown reason, the edition—some 500 copies in yellow paper covers—had never been distributed. It is not listed in MacLean's *Bibliography of Shaker Literature.*

It was an experience to happen upon a work that had been printed with a purpose in mind, but never used. The pamphlets were so clean, so bright in color, even on that dark and rainy day. And in opening one we were reminded of that poem by Robert Frost about the travelers who came upon an edition of poems, neglected and unread, in an abandoned farmhouse attic, and how the unknown poet must have rejoiced that, at long last, his work had found a reader.

XI

UNLEAVENED BREAD AND
SPIRITUAL CAKE

In old almanacs, commonplace books, and journals of the kitchen sisters, there are many recipes used in the Shaker cook-rooms and bake shops since the late eighteenth century. Some were brought in from the world, but many originated in the order itself, often a by-product of such industries as the dried sweet corn and herb. It has been fun to collect these documents.

Adding to the pleasure is the Shaker custom of injecting a bit of philosophy or religion into a recipe or pamphlet—as in the catalogue of chairs prepared for the Philadelphia Centennial in 1876, which included several Shaker hymns.

An example of this custom is a recipe for bread sent on request by Elder Frederick Evans of New Lebanon to a brother in Niskeyuna. The elder begins with the warning that the wheat must be *home-ground* and *coarse-ground.* "You might as well go to Moody and Sankey for pure Christianity," he writes, "as to go to a worldly miller with our wheat to grind." Beware also, he adds, of the fine ground or mercantile flour, "the leaven of the Pharisees." He continues, "I want something solid and substantial. I want to inherit substance—I want to see the redemption of the Stomach, redemption of the land; and the redemption of the creative forces of man and woman. The first step in the work of human redemption is to make and eat good bread."

Only after these preliminary remarks does the writer get around to the recipe itself:

1) Good clean wheat, coarse ground in a Centennial Hand Mill.
2) Scald one third of the flour in boiling milk. When cool, mix in the remaining two thirds of flour.
3) Mold lightly, with a little dry flour, adding a very little salt.
4) Bake in a hot oven, on the oven bottom.

Elder Frederick's ideas on what constitutes good bread exemplify the Shaker's concept of their faith as one combining science, religion and inspiration. Hygiene had a theological basis. Good craftsmanship was applied Christianity. When a contributor to *The Manifesto* writes on "Temporal and Spiritual Tools," when some obscure poet refers to Mother Ann as a carpenter hewing a crooked stick to make it "straight and squair," or when another composes a piece entitled "Spiritual Loom," we know what they mean. A further example of the habit of investing material things with spiritual qualities is the following anonymous poem which we found as a neatly written manuscript among some old papers. It is transcribed verbatim.

Spiritual Cake

1. As I have been informed of late,
   There's something in the shaker's cake
   That does make souls contented hear.
   I'll now unfold the matter clear,

   To all who have got eyes to see,
   I will unfold the mystery,
   And tell them plainly how to make
   And feast upon the shaker cake.

2. Tis called in scripture living bread
   Because it quickens from the dead,
   It saves the soul from sin & strife
   Tis therefore called the bread of life.

   Tis not much matter whats the name
   For lo in substance tis the same
   Some call it cake with tempting seed
   Tis that by which the soul is freed.

3. No human wisdom cannot scan
   How this suports the iner man
   And when the soul's freed thoroughly
   A carnal nature then must die.

   No earthly substance we employ,
   But just our inward peace & joy,
   Nor is it any natural yeast
   That gives us this continual feast.

4. First by an honest heart within
   Confessing & forsaking sin,
   Gives us a taist of this good cake
   This hidden manna we partake,

   Tis season'd with the seed of grace,
   Which strengthens us to run our race
   To quit all vain and earthly ties,
   And run that we may win the prize

5. This cake is raised with gospel leven
   In which we taist the joys of heaven
   Tis also baken with gospel fire,
   Of burning truth & pure desire.

   So when this precious cake we taste
   It is so holy pure & chaste,
   All earthly pleasures seems like dross
   So we can glory in the cross.

6. And these who do all sin forsake,
   May truly feast on this good cake
   We know it is from heaven designed
   For to adorn and feast the mind.

   It fills our souls with great delight,
   Tho tis to nature out of sight,
   It is a substance we enjoy
   Which death and hell cannot destroy

7. And when enqueres [inquirers] come to see,
   This cake is set before them free,
   And if they love it surely they
   Will quit their sins and want to stay

   But if the appetite is low,
   The stomach must be cleansed, we know
   For while they in the broad way rome
   Their souls will lothe the honney comb.

8. And when the sistom [system] is made clean
   From all thats base and foul within
   Ther'e able to desern the good
   And feast upon the heavenly food

   And if they slight this precious cake
   And our emetics will not take
   We give them up if they refuse
   To serve the master which they choose.

XII

THREE SHAKERESSES

It is always interesting to know why people dissent from majority opinion and why they join minority movements. Some of the Shaker beliefs in particular were so unusual—if not heretical—that one wonders what forces impelled individuals to become converts and then loyal participants in such an unworldly way of life. For some it was a matter of conviction, a way of salvation, dedication to an ideal. For others it was an escape from trouble—physical, marital or economic, and an avenue to peace and security. Motives were often mixed, and no generalization can be made. The story of each adherent would vary, in particulars if not in essentials.

The following sketches of three Shaker sisters, one from the North family, one from the South, and the third from the Church family in New Lebanon may throw some light on the circumstances of recruitment. It may illustrate, as well, how the individuality of the recruit, once he or she had become identified with the cause, was developed rather than atrophied or regimented by it. Shaker communitarianism presented an environment, a challenge, which seemed to bring out the innate faculties of its communicants.

But we include these sketches and the one in the following chapter for another reason—Sisters Rosetta, Sarah, Sadie and Alice were our staunch friends. They respected our work, and we respected them. Often as our activities assumed greater scope, we were encouraged by the fact that these sisters, who stood for Shakerism in its purest form, placed on our work the stamp of approval.

ROSETTA STEPHENS

One of the rare proselytizing missions of the United Society after the Civil War accounted for the coming to New Lebanon, in 1871, of Rosetta Stephens. In that year Elder Frederick Evans, after conferring with the noted spiritualist, Dr. James M. Peebles, decided to revisit his

Sister Rosetta Stephens

English homeland in the hope of recruiting members for an order which was then slowly declining in numbers, and if conditions were favorable, possibly establishing a branch of the society there.

Soon after their arrival a meeting was held in St. George's Hall, London, presided over by Hepworth Dixon, the author of *New America* and attended by distinguished journalists, members of Parliament, clergymen, spiritualists and secularists. Elder Frederick was the chief speaker, an "inspired" man it was said that day, as he extolled in a clear and strong voice the virtues of Shakerism, and boldly criticized England's "sins and shortcomings." Women, he suggested in passing, should take their place in the clergy and hereditary nobility in the House of Lords.

In the audience was Rosetta's father, a paisley shawl designer and weaver, who had been forced to leave Manchester and move to London because of his radical opposition to the Crimean War. Here he had become the manager of a group of cooperative stores, a position providing an outlet for his strongly socialistic interests. He was also one of the founders of the "Humanitarian Brotherhood," which stood for the "fraternal distributive principle" as opposed to the "individual accumulative one." It was small wonder then that this particular Seeker was an entranced listener to the gospel of communitarianism. He decided to come to America and accepted the Elder's proposal that his daughter visit, as a probationer, the novitiate order at New Lebanon. Rosetta, her stepbrother, and a few others were the first fruits of Evans' mission. She was then eleven years old.

Many incidents of interest occurred during the elder's stay in London. One worth recalling, for the light it sheds on the eccentricities of some of the Believers, pertains to the "fashionable" breakfast to which he and Dr. Peebles were invited the morning after the St. George's address. Before Evans left his lodging (Peebles later wrote) he took from his trunk a good-sized chunk of coarse ground, unleavened Shaker bread, and putting it in his satchel, started off for the engagement. Ten or twelve guests were awaiting the visitors in an elegantly appointed room. On arriving, the tall, "reverential-looking" elder took out his bread, "half as large as a quart bowl," and sitting down at the table, laid it by his plate. As the honored guest, he was asked to say grace. "Crossing his hands and sitting as erect as a towering pine, Evans said: 'In my accustomed way.'" His way was "as silent as the depths of silence itself." Not a word from his lips! "Soon there was passed him a cup of coffee. He did not take coffee. 'Do you prefer tea, or cocoa?' 'Nay,' said the Elder, 'I take neither.' There was passed to him a plate of fish. 'Nay,' said he, 'I do not take fish.' 'Perhaps you would prefer steak.' 'Nay, I do not take steak, or any animal flesh.' 'Well, really, Elder,' his hosts insisted, 'what do you eat and drink?' 'I drink water when thirsty,' Frederick replied, 'and I brought my bread with me, for I did not expect to find any London bakers' bread that was fit to eat.' "

This exchange opened the way, Peebles recalled, for a two-hour discussion on vegetarianism and the importance of pure, wholesome food in physical and mental health.

Rosetta's life at the North family or Gathering Order followed the uneventful but industrious course of all the Shaker sisterhood. She was devoted to Elder Frederick and Eldress Antoinette Doolittle, the spiritual heads of the family, and to their successors, Eldresses Anna White and Leila Taylor. She was free to leave, to join her father and stepmother, who had settled in New Jersey, or to return to England, but once established in her peaceful mountain home she had no desire to depart. Domestic duties in the kitchen, retiring rooms, laundry and cannery; shop duties, the making of shirts, rug weaving, the manufacture of carpet whips, etc.; religious duties and social obligations, of which there were many as this was the reception center for visitors and prospective members—all these varied activities kept her contented in spirit. Her greatest interest was music. Many Shaker hymns and anthems, both text and notation, were from her gifted pen, in addition to contributions for *The Manifesto,* the monthly organ of the society. Often these were poems, and one of our cherished manuscripts was one she wrote for us in February, 1933:

On receiving an ivy-leaf from Westminster Abbey.

As clings the ivy unto ruins old,
So to my heart fond memories ever cling,
& down the aisles of years faint, distant voices ring;
I tread again that spectral silence cold,
See cenotaphs and urns and arches bold.

The chancel light reveals each cloistered thing,
The sacred shrine of prophet, bard and king,
A treasure-house of riches, manifold.
And so I tread the vast sepulchral gloom,
Mid trophies proud that chronicle high fame,
The dust of kings that lies in sculptured tomb,
Shall vanish and forgotten be their name;
But souls that spoke for God, we all adore,
The kings of *mind* shall live forever more.

On the death of Eldress Ella Winship in 1940, Sister Rosetta's long consecration was rewarded by her elevation first to eldress and then to the central ministry of the United Society.

The spirit of her nunlike Shaker life was that of Anna Hempstead Branch's "The Monk in the Kitchen," who, believing there was "no small work unto God," sang of simplicity, of lowly grace, and of order as a lovely thing:

> Whoever makes a thing more bright,
> He is an angel of all light,
> Therefore let me spread abroad
> The beautiful cleanness of my God.

SARAH COLLINS

Van Wyck Brooks' character Oliver Allston, like the poet Leopardi, believed that the value of a civilization was determined by "the amount of the singularity one finds among the people of the country." For this reason he rejoiced in the Shakers: in the variety of character there to be found, the "biblical pattern" of their minds, their "classical modes" of living, the color they gave to the "human landscape." Certainly Oliver would have enjoyed meeting Sarah Collins. When we first made her acquaintance in the South family chair shop, Sister Sarah had been a member of the order for over sixty years. Still, she had preserved and developed that singularity of character which made her more widely known to the world, perhaps, than any other member of the sect. To hundreds of visitors at the South, Second and North families, where she successively lived, Sarah epitomized Shakerism without loss of that engaging, almost eccentric individualism which was her special charm.

This last survivor of the South family was born in Boston, probably in 1855. She never knew, she said, how old she was, and had only the dimmest memories of her parents and two brothers. Her father never returned from the Civil War, and her mother died during that conflict. When she was seven years old, she was brought to New Lebanon through the efforts of Dr. John Milton Brewster, a public-spirited physician of Pittsfield, and Elder Daniel Hawkins of the Second family. Elder Daniel, a lover of children, a "real saint" whose good deeds Sarah never tired of extolling, had consented to take the lead of the South Order (at that time a branch of the Second family) on condition that a "class" of boys and girls be formed there. Sister Sarah was a member of the first group.

There, in 1862, she began her long lifework, attending the school taught by Sister Emily Smith, making the cushion pads used in the chair seats, helping in the cheese and sweet corn industries, worshipping with song and dance at the Saturday and Sabbath Meetings, and for recreation wandering over the Taconic hills for berries. Tall and lean, black-haired and sunken-eyed, restless, tireless, there was something of the Indian about her. "Tough as a pine knot," she used to say. When she was past eighty, a bout of pneumonia forced her to go to the hospital.

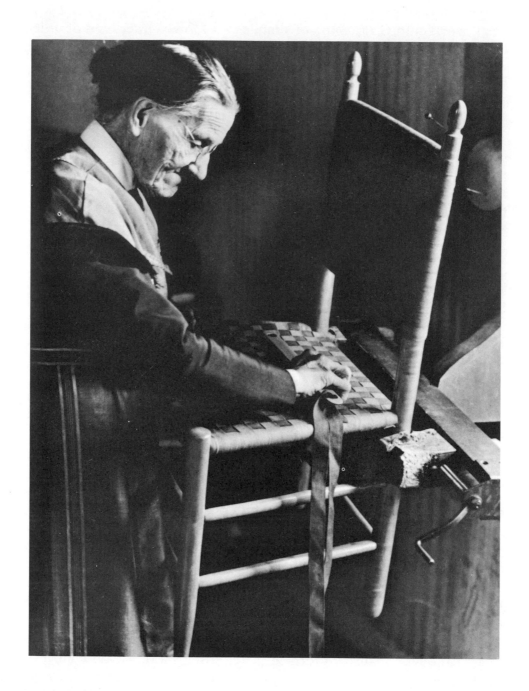

Sister Sarah Collins

The experience upset her. "What happened?" she wondered after her return—"I never had a moment's sickness before." And soon after her eighty-seventh birthday, on one of our last visits (she was braiding a large rug, with a cat asleep in a rocker nearby) she insisted she still could "run like a deer—except it would scare the cat!"

Under such leaders as Elder Hawkins, Eldress Polly Lewis and Elder Robert Wagan, Sister Sarah found enough to keep her physical energy and social instincts abundantly engaged. The South family was just beginning a period of great enterprise, reviving on a large scale a chair-making business whose origins, among the Shakers, went back to the 1780's. In 1863, the year after she arrived at the settlement, the South family, then an independent order of forty members, became the exclusive manufacturers of chairs, selling its product to other families and societies and to the world. The wholesaling of chairs, foot benches, "turning stools," etc. to city dealers began about 1868, increasing so fast that four years later a new factory had to be built and a trademark adopted as a protection against imitation and competition. Representatives of firms from New York, Boston and as far west as Chicago and Racine, Wisconsin, as well as visitors who began to hear of the product through newspaper advertisements, the exhibits at the Philadelphia Centennial in 1876, and other sources, came to the settlement in increasing numbers, with little diminution till the chair shop closed.

Such guests were always hospitably received: it was Sister Sarah's role, when she was not seating chairs or dyeing the frames, to assist in the preparation of meals and the accommodation of these "world's people." Her days were never too busy, however, to exclude the amenities. She loved to talk—small talk, tall talk, all talk. Possessed of a remarkable memory for names and faces as well as a special affection for children, Sister Sarah was known far and wide, to young and old. Her sense of recognition was almost intuitive. Once, when we were there, a mother carrying a baby came into the shop. Sarah stopped her work and glanced quizzically at the little one. "You're a Connecticut baby, aren't you?" she asked. And she was right.

Many stories have been told about this colorful Shakeress. Another is worth recalling. Sarah was once visiting a friend who had in her garden a plaster statue of a Greek goddess. One misty morning, early—it was Shaker custom to rise at 4:30—her hostess noticed her out in the garden looking at the statue, and taking out her handkerchief lean over and carefully wipe off a drop of dew from the end of the goddess's nose!

She was a natural "mother in Israel," her kindness all-embracing. No beggar was ever turned away without food and a night's shelter, the "tramp house" at the South family being the last so used in all the Shaker colonies.

After the deaths of Elder Robert and the patriarchal William Anderson, Sister Sarah carried on the chair business in her own inimitable way. With a stubby pencil she would scratch out the orders on any piece of paper that was handy, pin to it a sample of the tape which the customer had selected, and put the scrap on a tall spindle on her cluttered table. Though it would seem, therefore, that the last orders would be the first to be filled, she usually met the promised date.

An unforgettable person. We can see her again, bending over a chair attached by a frame to the wall, pulling tight the tapes, rush, or splint—hard work often carried on into the twilight; or standing on the "bridge" connecting her second-floor shop with the store-room, a point of vantage from which she could survey her world and have foreknowledge of arrivals. Her fingers were twisted like tree roots, whether from arthritis or the long years of seating chairs she herself did not know. Her ill-fitting set of "store teeth" was a concession to appearances; usually lying on a counter amidst thread, tape and tools, they would be clapped into her mouth on the approach of a visitor. Perhaps her small, gold-rimmed glasses were also a concession, for she always looked *over* them, keenly but amicably. Her hair was still dark, her wiry figure still clad in Shaker butternut or indigo cloth.

An early Believer, Sarah loved to sing such traditional songs as:

> Come life, Shaker life,
> Come life eternal,
> Shake, shake out of me
> All that is carnal.
> I'll take nimble steps,
> I'll be a David,
> I'll show Michael twice
> How he behaved!

Singing such songs, she would be oblivious to the present. Taking "nimble steps" up and down the room, she would begin to shake—an involuntary "operation" starting with the shoulders and then enveloping the arms and body—in what was called the "back manner" of early Shaker worship.

In a peculiar way, Sarah Collins lived in both the past and the present. The place which was her home for eighty years was originally the Bishop farm where Mother Ann Lee in 1780 conducted, in an orchard back of the house, the first Shaker service in New Lebanon. It is fitting that this shrine of Shakerism should have been the spot where one of its last devotees lived, deep into the twentieth century, a life which was truly representative of an archaic biblical faith.

The young Neale sisters, Emma (left) and Sadie

SADIE NEALE
A Shaker "Forty-niner"

It was evening on the third day of December, 1855, when two little girls, six and eight years of age, came over the South Mountain for the first time. The evening was dark, but the ground was covered with snow and the sleighing good; so it did not take long for a sprightly team to carry these children, with their foster parents, to their destination on the heights of the Lebanon hills overlooking a beautiful valley below.

So begin the reminiscences of a Shaker sister who, during the twenty years or so of our acquaintance, represented for us the essential virtues of Shakerism. Born in 1849, Sadie Neale loved to call herself a "forty-niner". She lived to be ninety-eight, surviving by two years her sister Emma, who had been her companion on that wintry ride from Williamstown, Massachusetts, to New Lebanon, New York, so long ago.

Sister Sadie in the early 1930's

The impact of Sister Sadie's life on ours may best be explained in terms of character—character which had matured in the testing and shaping of over nine decades of service to a cause in which she profoundly believed. Though she was over seventy-five when we first met her, her work even then was far from finished. At ninety she was tending a post office, managing a shop for the sale of boxes and other handicraft, supervising the farm of the Church "family", planning a new orchard. She was fulfilling in these labors, as in others, the dictum of Mother Ann Lee, the founder of the Shaker society, "to do your work as though you had a thousand years to live, and as you would if you were to die tomorrow."

Hers was a life of incessant and varied industry. In that remote ante-bellum December, the indenture agreement having been signed between her foster parents and the Shaker trustees, Sadie was placed in the Children's Order, where she attended the communal school and learned, in common with the other children, an occupation suitable to her years but useful in the sect's economy. Her first task was the braiding of palm leaf for the table mats in which a large business was then conducted. From this she graduated to the bonnet industry, weaving on a small Shaker-made loom the straw braids with which the front edges of the bonnets were bound. As she grew older, weaving remained a central interest. She cherished the miniature loom which had been her introduction, at eight years of age, into an order which enjoined all "to put their hands to work, and their hearts to God." Often we found her at a larger loom, alone in some quiet shop, weaving a strip of cloth. Her love for the art was such that it often found voice in her writings. "The warp of life is long and the filling fine," was her philosophy, "and the whole fabric appears not at one time."

When still in her teens, Sadie was sent to the Watervliet society, where she served as teacher of the North family school, combining her duties with those of assistant to Elder George Lomas, editor of the monthly journal, *The Shaker,* which made its first appearance in 1871. The occasional contributions of the young Shakeress to this periodical are indices of a keen mind—a mind which was being molded by the communal traditions of usefulness, constructive labor, and the importance of action in the development of character. She wrote in a piece called "Flowers and Their Uses" that, "All things are intended to be made useful. Those who have a natural love for flowers . . . are fortunate to have discovered that while nearly all call them beautiful, they are truly subjects for use"—in the education of children, in the sick-room, in the cultivation of the life of the spirit. Discussing the uses of failure, she noted in another article that "the road to success leads through a country of failures." But if one truly labors to win, failure forms the incentive for renewed effort, and attainment will be realized, even though it be "after this life's ultimate."

A third contribution epitomized a philosophy to which Sadie was true for seventy years after it was written. "Character," she wrote, "is eternal, living when all finite forms turn to dust. Like principle, it maintains a positive indifference to all things save facts and realities. It cannot be formed, it cannot be improved except through *action*, except as one *does* something." An ideal untranslated into action is a barren, useless thing. Sister Sadie was never so impatient as with indolence and inefficiency in others, scornfully declaring in a favorite phrase of hers, "you can't turn off what has never been turned on."

In the early 1880's she returned to the New Lebanon community to become mistress of the recently established Shaker post office, a position she was holding when we first knew her. We can still see her, a diminutive figure in butternut-dyed Shaker dress and straw bonnet, intently sorting and distributing the mail in the old brick office, completely isolated from all other concerns. She would glance up as we entered, her eyes twinkling a welcome behind her steel-rimmed glasses; but we knew that our business must wait until she had finished her appointed task. "One world at a time," she would often say, and "Order is heaven's first law."

"Our business" was the collecting of Shakeriana: furniture, small joinery, fabrics, basketry, tools and domestic utensils, books, manuscripts, songs, prints, stories—anything which was the product of this productive order. And in this undertaking Sadie soon became a key figure. The Shakers had lived apart from the world for a century and a half, and, holding themselves aloof, were suspicious of strangers whose visits were often motivated by mere curiosity. But once assured of the sincerity of the motive, no people could be more friendly. Our objective was nothing less than the documentation and interpretation of an incomparably rich native culture. And when Sadie was once convinced on this score, she gave without stint of herself and her great knowledge. As the leading family in the central community, the Church at New Lebanon was a treasure-house of "facts and realities." To the fine workmanship of the Believers and the basic sources of their traditions we were provided access, just before it was too late, by a devotee who longed to transmit to others the heritage of her people.

Her transmitting was a blend of generosity and spirituality. Each act was a happy one elevated by intelligent purpose. Every visit was an experience. We would spend hours rummaging through old abandoned shops, attics, storerooms and basements, picking up innumerable items—some handmade tool or labor-saving device, an oval box perhaps, a packet of herb labels or a package of herbs, perhaps a chair or a stand, whatever had meaning as a product of Shaker hands.

Sadie had a shrewd sense of value. But she was generous almost to a fault. For collections of what might be called the minutiae of labor, a basket of odds and ends, a box of choice little pieces of this and that, the price was often a nominal one. "Trumpery!" she would say, half disdainfully, wrinkling her nose and shutting her eyes in a way she had.

Often we found her, in the spring, engaged in some phase of gardening or orcharding—she had the title, at one time, of "orchard deaconess." Scenes come into our memories that are like pictures, interiors like those of the Flemish masters: one, for instance, of Sadie in a cool basement kitchen, trimming the stems from a generous bunch of asparagus and tying them neatly with a pink tape; another of a shop in a disused herb house, a room flooded with spring sunshine, where, seated in an old slat-back chair and surrounded by baskets heaped to overflowing, she used to dispense her crop of cherries. The planning and growing, the harvesting and selling of the fruits of the earth were to her, as to all true Believers, a ritual. The earth was a sphere to be redeemed; to increase its fertility was a religious service; to sell only the best (keeping anything inferior for home use) was a "millennial" law.

The Shaker husbandman was more preoccupied with service than with profit. Receiving the gardener's yield—be it asparagus or cherries, sweet corn, potatoes, or Northern Spy apples—seemed less like a business transaction, therefore, than participation in a sort of sacrament of the seasons. A lady from the world was once visiting the Neale sisters. She was shown about the office by Emma, who was a trustee, and as such, concerned about family finances, aspects of which she discussed with the visitor. Inquiring whether there was any garden produce for sale, she was turned over to Sadie, and in the course of conversation mentioned Emma's remarks about money. "Humpfh!" said Sadie, wrinkling her nose, "Emma's commercial, I'm agricultural."

On inclement days, and as she grew less active physically, Sadie was usually to be found in her retiring room, seated under a window on a sort of dais (a platform called a "throne," large enough for a chair and sewing desk) which provided better light for sewing and reading, and a wide western view of the Lebanon Valley she loved. After a few remarks on weather, health and the news of the day, the conversation invariably turned Shaker. Once, we recall, as we were discussing the dance-songs which were an integral part of the worship of the sect, she descended from her "throne," her cheeks aglow and her eyes alight, to demonstrate for us the shuffling steps, the bowings and turnings of the old song, "The Gift to be Simple:"

> Tis the gift to be simple,
> Tis the gift to be free,
> Tis the gift to come down

Where we ought to be—
And when we find ourselves
In the place just right,
Twill be in the valley
Of love and delight.

When true simplicity is gained,
To bow and to bend
We shan't be ashamed,
To turn, turn will be our delight,
Till by turning, turning
We *come round right.*

With a final whirl, we can see her now stamping out the three steps which marked the last three words of the song, and returning excited and breathless to her chair.

Another memorable event occurred the day we told her of the impending razing of the Hancock meeting-house, on the other side of the mountain. The assembly room of this building, the scene of the ceremonial dances of that society, was lined with blue pegboards and Indian-red benches: the panelled window frames and doors were intact; the windows and doors, with their hand-wrought iron fixtures, were in as good structural condition as when the house was built in 1786. We longed to see it saved, but the asking price, though small, was beyond our means. We put the problem before our Shaker friend. Talk went on, and the subject changed. But just before we left, Sadie recurred to the issue. "It is true," she remarked, "that most institutions, the United Society not excepted, follow a cycle of birth, growth, decline and passage." But since the Shakers had made so important a contribution to the social and economical development of America, any act of preservation was a duty to history—one way, she believed, of transmitting something of "our work" to posterity. She wanted to be of help in the present instance, whereupon she brought forth, from beneath her Shaker cot, a box in which she kept the receipts from her handicraft shop. Rummaging through it she took out some bills, and after carefully placing them in an envelope, quietly, proudly, entrusted them to us. And so it happened, through this act of faith, that the assembly room was saved.

While cherishing the past and living to the full in the present, our benefactress was forever projecting herself into the future. More than all else she wanted the Shaker work to go on: as example, as inspiration, as part of the historic process. She would have agreed with us, we are sure, that collecting artifacts of whatever sort—no matter how valuable and beautiful thay may be—just as objects in themselves does not in the end, afford the fullest satisfaction. One wanted to know *why* these things were made, their uses in context, the secrets of style, something of the thought of the maker. Often we talked with Sadie about the doctrines of the Shakers and the principles of their temporal economy, and through her instrumentality we acquired a considerable part of our library. One day, as we were discussing such matters, she became strangely quiet and distracted, then told us she had a document which she wanted us to have. Going over to a box by her bedside in which she kept farm accounts, memorabilia and other papers, she extracted, after some search, a manuscript booklet with a faded blue cover. It was the original Shaker covenant, signed in 1795 by the founders of the New Lebanon Church!

Having to spend our winters away from the Believers, we saw less and less of Sadie during the last few years of her life. Occasionally a letter arrived, composed in a steady hand. In one, during war time (1942), she was gravely concerned about the state of the world: "Our earth seems to have gone off on a tangent (she wrote) and no one seems to know where it has gone. Our centripetal and centrifugal forces seem to have crossed each other in an unexplainable way." In another was a poem:

> Foxes had their rest and the birds their nest
> In the shade of the cedar tree,
> But the Son of God had no place for his head
> In the regions of Galilee.

Her final letter to us, date of April 5, 1945, was written in her same steady hand, though she was then ninety-six years old. It was an account of simple matters:

> Dear Friends:
> Yours was duly received, and was not I pleased. We had a very pleasant Easter, but a very quiet one. No one came to see and we went to see no one—but we were happy among ourselves . . . We may have some setbacks but we can put up with these. We cannot expect to have anything settled, even the weather, while the country is in its present condition. Some are talking Peace, but I do not see it yet . . . Roberts is still making (oval) boxes for me when he can get material to work with . . . But I am nearing the end of my journey and shall not miss these things much longer . . . I hope to see you once more. Now as I have nothing more (worth) writing about, I will love you and leave you in peace . . . ever yours
> Affectionately
> Sadie

We saw her once more, one chill autumn day soon after the last members of the Lebanon colony had been moved to Hancock. Sadie was sitting, bundled in a cloak, in the waning sunlight of a western doorway. She was feeble, confined to her chair, and it was hard for her to hear. But somehow one did not think of her as an invalid—though her work was done, her spirit was unchanged and seemed unchangeable.

When the news of her death came, we thought of the times when, in her indigo blue dress and bonnet and black Shaker cape, she had attended the funeral of some sister or brother, dignifying, indeed glorifying the occasion by her presence. In her slight figure and serene countenance there was such strength that the onlooker felt in his heart: "There is no death here."

We were sure that Sister Sadie Neale, the forty-niner, the active searcher for spiritual gold, was not in useless mourning at her own funeral.

XIII

A SHAKER SISTER AND
HER INSPIRATIONALS

The early June evening is mild
and diffused with a softly blowing mist.
A half moon sheds through broken clouds
A gentle light on the laundry house
Rising high and narrow and mystically white
Into the drifting sky.
A whippoorwill off to the north
Calls its faint note in the Taconic woods.
Then nearer, suddenly, by the church
Across the way.
A Shaker sister kneels on a garden path
To show us opening blooms,
Crickets sound incessantly low,
And we are shrouded in endless peace.

E.D.A.

The sister kneeling on the garden path was one of those true Believers who earnestly desired to conserve what was pure in the heritage of the society—and pass it on. She lived in that latter day when the culture was becoming adulterated by alien elements, a neglect of or indifference to those principles on which the order had been founded. She believed that Hancock would be the community to last the longest, and this being so, that she had a special mission to make it deserving of the trust. Often she must have been discouraged, for she was not physically well, and there was nobody left in the family with whom she could share her thoughts. She was waiting, it seemed, for someone else who cared.

Our friendship with Alice Smith was one of those pure experiences which, in anyone's lifetime, are rare indeed. She had a great gift and a great need for friendship. Her face and dark eyes, sad in repose, would light up, and her whole personality awaken when we would drop in for a visit. We might find her anywhere in the village: working in the cook-room or wash house, weaving on the big carpet loom in the weave shop, tending the flower garden, sewing in her retiring room, or tidying up somewhere on the three expansive floors of the Church family dwelling. Whatever she was doing she would stop to give us her time. Our visits became longer and more frequent.

Her gift to be creative found expression in a white-walled room of the sisters' shop which she had furnished and where I worked during several summers on my furniture book. It was here that we three entertained our special guests. Whether aglow with sunlight or softly lit by candles, the room had a serenity that was balm to the spirit, affecting beneficently all that transpired there.

We remember, too, the many picnics in the "rock orchard" beyond the round stone barn; the teas at our home in Pittsfield when Alice might bring certain Shaker sisters of whom she was particularly fond; the delightful evenings at Hanna Farm in Interlaken where the Berkshire Music Festival had its beginning. We recall the days when she would take us into nooks and crannies of the big dwelling at Hancock, from the cellar with its marble floor and arched brick doorways to the upper lofts, to look at pieces of furniture or other articles which had been tucked away. She had grown up with these things. She loved them for their own sake, and often for their association with some person in the family. But she was willing to sell, in the interests both of preservation and need. The anxious weeks when she stayed at our house after a serious operation are still acutely recalled.

Most memorable of all were our intimate talks in Alice's retiring room. There she could be herself. There she disclosed matters close to her heart. She had put away in secret places things that she had kept or rescued ever since the years when, as a girl, she and her sister Ethel were placed in the order by their father. Among these treasures was a small collection of the beautifully "pricked" manuscript hymnals in which the early songs of the Believers were recorded. Alice loved music, played the organ, and could recall the time when Shakers still sang and danced in their worship. The hymnals were a link with the past. But the future, too, was important, and the time came when she showed us her precious song-books, and then, not long afterwards, gave them to us—to form the nucleus of our own collection.

The hymnals were a revelation, though we knew such books existed. More remarkable and a complete surprise was another treasure which Sister Alice had hidden away. How unforgettable is the day when she told us there was something in her "hope chest" which she wanted us to see. Whereupon she brought out from an anteroom a carefully wrapped scroll, some two feet long, and unrolled it for our inspection.

What we saw was the first of those mysterious paintings which we

Sister Alice Smith

have come to call "inspirationals." We were totally unaware at the time of the existence of such documents. We lacked words to express our thoughts. Spellbound, we gazed at the rows of faces bordered by trees, flowers and other emblems and surmounted by arcs representing clouds, all in color—"A Vision," so the inscription read, "of the Heavenly Sphere."

When we had recovered from our amazement Alice told us this story. When she was a little girl helping in the kitchen, she noticed that an eldress, during the spring cleaning season, was putting under the fuel log in the bake oven a roll of papers with many colored and pen-and-ink designs. There were floral and arboreal symbols and various decorations which had no meaning to her, but which she instinctively realized had charm. She begged the eldress to let her have them, and when the request was granted she took the bundle to her own room, adding them to other things which she had collected. As she grew older, and studied the documents, more and more she came to realize they had a special significance. Yet she hesitated to show them to anyone, in the family or out, knowing that the Shakers themselves feared they might be ridiculed. Indeed, in many cases they had been destroyed.

Showing this one painting to us, Sister Alice confessed, was to be a test. If we found it "amusing" or a subject for idle curiosity, she had made up her mind to destroy it along with the others she hinted at possessing. She felt that if we, as world's people she was beginning to trust, failed to perceive any beauty or intrinsic meaning in them, they should never go out into the world.

Now the "Vision of the Heavenly Sphere" was ours to cherish, and to interpret as best we could. Other inspirationals came to us in due course, sealing, as it were, our devotion to the beloved sister and the ideal to which she had devoted her life.

Not long afterwards Sister Alice passed away. Elsewhere we have told about her funeral, but there is more to tell. It was a cold early spring morning. The little band of Hancock Shakers, with their sisters and brethren from over the mountain and a few from other communities, was assembled in the meeting-room of the dwelling. As was the custom, after a hymn and a prayer, anyone was free to speak. We recall the moving testimonies of Sisters Sadie and Rosetta. Though we were of the world, we could not remain silent. So we added our own tribute, words uttered in sorrow but deep sincerity:

> The person for whom we are assembled here today found her life, at an early age, identified with a certain faith. I think we should recall at this time with what profound seriousness, yet with what a bright spirit, she undertook the responsibilities of this her

calling, how she grew in understanding, how finally she saw, with deepest insight, the essential good in Shakerism and the importance of conserving that good and projecting it, in all ways possible, into the future. She returned, in her constant thought to the ideals held by the early Believers, having faith that these ideals were yet alive. Intelligently but humbly she labored, with her hands and in the subtle ways of the spirit, for the constructive good of the order, feeling that the fate that had placed her in the community had assigned to her an appointed work. How well she accomplished her mission, with what unselfish devotion, we all must know. Through her spirit, many from the world caught the inspiration she held, gaining through her personality an appreciation of the Shaker life at its best, and a glimpse of the vision of brotherhood, beauty and consecrated industry for which the order stood. This vision has a timeless quality. The spirit which we have come to know as Sister Alice was a personification of this vision, and as such transcends death. Precious is this soul, and undying.

XIV

AN UPRIGHT MAN OF GOD

The Shaker mission to England in 1887 did not add many new members to the order. Rosetta Stephens was one of the few. But it served to publicize one of the most dynamic and controversial leaders of nineteenth century Shakerism. We did not know Elder Frederick W. Evans in person. But we knew Believers who had known him and were aware that his personality must have been a strong one. The world considered him the spokesman of the movement.

I am not sure he was that, or that he was universally admired within the society. For one thing, he was too outspoken. Though he once wrote that he could see "great importance in a principle, very little in an individual," his opinions were so vigorous and his manner so stern and commanding that his individuality could not be effaced. He was, I suspect, an egocentric. His interpretation of Shakerism was a personalized one, not always true to the principles set forth by the early leaders. On the other hand we have the testimony of respected members of the North family in New Lebanon—people like Eldress Antoinette Doolittle, Eldress Anna White, Sister Martha Anderson and Elder Daniel Offord—that though he was "firm and radical in opinion" he was "a noble and upright man of God."

His career was a remarkable one. Born in Leominster, Worchestershire, England on June 9, 1808, he was sent to school at Stourbridge at the age of four. As the "poorest scholar" there, he was released from the hated school books and the "flogging proclivities" of the schoolmaster. At eight he was sent to live with uncles and aunts at Chadwick Hall, near Licky Hill. Here his associates were almost exclusively the servants, and his education was "reading and studying" the vegetables and fruits, the land and its crops, the farm animals and the great outdoors. On Sunday he was taken to the Episcopal church, where he learned the Collect.

When Frederick was twelve years old, his father and brother George visited Chadwick Hall to ask the boy whether he preferred to remain there or go with them to America. All that he knew about this strange country was the doggerel, dating from Revolutionary times, which he had heard the common people still singing:

> The sun will burn your nose off,
> And the frost will freeze your toes off,
> But we must away,
> To fight our friends and relatives
> In North America.

Adventuresome in spirit and healthy in body, the boy eagerly agreed to go. So the year 1820 found him on board the ship *Favorite,* laden with salt and iron, bound from Liverpool to New York, the same route that Mother Ann Lee had taken nearly a half century before. And like the ship *Mariah* on which she had sailed, the passage was also a rough one. The ship sprang a leak and all hands were ordered to the pump.

From New York the party went to Newburgh, and then by team to Binghamton, where two uncles had settled. For ten years or so this was Frederick's home. Here he took "a sudden turn in respect to books and learning," starting in with the *Life of Nelson* and continuing with the Bible. While still in his teens he placed himself under the tutelage of an Episcopal minister in Ithaca, where he had access to a library and avidly read Plutarch, *The Tatler* and *The Spectator,* Shakespeare, Young, Watts, Plato and Rollins' *Ancient History.* The *Koran* and other religious works awakened an interest in theology, but made him wonder why he was a Christian rather than a Moslem or a follower of Confucius. Then, on reading Volney, Voltaire and Paine's *Crisis* and *The Rights of Man,* foundations were laid for a belief in materialism and socialism.

The 1820's were years of social unrest and radical political ideas. The forces were rife which brought Jackson into the presidency, at the same time advancing the socialistic theories of Robert Owen and Fourier. Frederick became associated with his brother George in the publication of *The Workingman's Advocate, The Daily Sentinal* and *Young America,* at the masthead of which was printed their platform:

The right of man to the soil
Down with monopolies, especially the United States Bank
Freedom of the public lands
Inalienable homesteads
Abolition of laws for the collection of debts
A general bankrupt law
A lien of the labourer upon his own work for his wages
Abolition of imprisonment for debt
Equal rights of women with men in all respects
Abolition of chattel slavery and wage slavery
Land limitation to 160 acres per individual
Mails to run on the Sabbath

The reformers gradually gained strength, and on the evening of October 29, 1825, at a stormy meeting in Tammany Hall, the radicals outvoted the conservatives, who revengefully turned off the gas. The reformers thus acquired, by lighting locofoco matches to candles, the name of the Locofoco Party. (There was either a lapse of memory on the part of Evans in his *Autobiography* or a typographical error in the date. The meeting was in 1834 and the party was organized in 1835.)

In 1828, seeking the ideal community in which he could give practical expression to his socialistic convictions, Frederick had walked eight hundred miles from New York to join the Owenite society at Massilon, Ohio, the short-lived Kendall Community. Here he found many kindred "infidel" spirits, but also some Christians, whom he considered the cause of the breakup of that community soon after his arrival. In consequence he and a number of other utopians planned to form a "philosophical society" which would not admit a single Christian.

Apparently the project never materialized. In 1829, at any event, we find the young seeker journeying down the Ohio River to Cincinnati, and thence by flatboat to New Orleans, where he witnessed at first hand the evils of chattel slavery.

After a trip to England and back, Frederick became active in the Hall of Science in New York, where he became acquainted with Robert Dale Owen and Fanny Wright. Still interested in forming a secular community, he was deputized to investigate various communitarian experiments in the country, and it was on such a mission that he called one day in the month of June, 1830, at the North family, or Novitiate Order, at New Lebanon.

Here a miracle occurred. Though Evans had heard that the Shakers were the "most ignorant and fanatical people in existence," he was impressed by their "air of candor and openness," and by the fact that they deplored the same evils in the world that he had denounced. In fact, he paid them the compliment of calling them a society of infidels. In the Shaker order, he discovered, there were no laws for the collection of debts, for there were no debts. Women were accorded the same rights and given the same responsibilities as men. As a materialist Evans relied upon evidence, of the mind, of the senses; he noted that the Shakers practiced what they taught. "Their whole life was a religious one; all their temporal, no less than their spiritual affairs, being the exponent of their religion."

There was a sensory element, however, in Frederick's conversion. It was not by "the power of argument," he later testified, but by certain mystical manifestations received during his stay at the Shaker family. By offering indisputable evidence, these convinced him that there was a spiritual sphere, an inner world more substantial than the outer one:

Frederick Wm. Evans

One night, soon after retiring [he recalled], I heard a rustling sound, as of the wind of a flock of doves flying through the window [which was closed] towards my bed; and, that I believed it to be supernatural, and that the faith in the supernatural, which the servants [in England] had planted in my soul, by their oft-told ghost stories, had not wholly died out under my materialism, was evidenced by the fact that I was frightened, and hid my head beneath the bed-clothes. . . . I soon recovered my self-possession, and found that a singular mental phenomenon was going on. I was positively *illuminated*. My reasoning powers were enhanced a hundred-fold. I could see a chain of problems, or propositions, as in a book, all spread out before me at once, starting from a fact that I *did* admit and believe; and leading me, step by step, mathematically, to a given conclusion, which I had *not* hitherto believed. I then discovered that I had powers within me that I knew not of. I was multiplied and magnified, and intensely interested. Doubting was at a discount; for here were facts, something of which my senses were cognizant—my physical, mental, rational, and spiritual senses; and I *knew* that intelligences not clothed in what I had called *matter* were present with me . . . This first visitation of angels to me continued till one o'clock in the morning, having lasted several hours.

The next night they came again. This time it was spirit acting upon matter. Something began at my feet, and operated as palpably as water, or fire, or electricity; but it was neither; to me it was a new force, or element, or power—call it what you please . . . . It passed quite slowly upward throughout my whole body. These visitations recurred nightly for three weeks, always different, always kind and pleasant . . . showing me the facts of the existence of a spiritual world, of the immortality of the human soul, and of the possibility and reality of intercommunication between souls in and spirits out of the mortal body.

At the end of three weeks, conviction of the reality of the spiritual world came upon him, and he said to himself, "It is enough." And from that moment the manifestations ceased.

After a brief visit to his friends at the Hall of Science Frederick returned to New Lebanon to become a Shaker. There he remained for the rest of his life, devoting his exceptional talents to a cause to which he had been mysteriously converted. These talents were versatile. He had learned the hatting business during a stay at Shelburne Four Corners, N.Y. He was as much at home in the shops and fields as in the meeting house, where for decades he was the public preacher, or in his study, where he wrote his cogently reasoned tracts on social and political reform. From his early experience in England he could discourse with authority on such matters as ensilage, stock raising, or the proper manner of planting fruit trees. He became a vegetarian, with strong opinions on diet and hygiene. In support of the principle of non-resistance he interviewed Lincoln, and after the Civil War welcomed Secretary of War Stanton to the Shaker village. His correspondents included Henry George and Leo Tolstoy.

Many of Evans' ideas were relevant to the problems of our own day. In a work on *Shaker Communism,* for instance, in discussing the issue of overpopulation, he noted that though "all the faculties of man were originally good and innocent, not excepting that of procreation," man had been led to corrupt them "by making *pleasure,* not *use,* the end of their action and exercise." In Evans' mind, as in Shaker doctrine, this was lust. An advocate of the celibate principle for those who were called and able to lead the divine life, he nevertheless did not condemn marriage, and like Mother Ann, urged the world to have fewer and better children.

"Always so to live, that I could respect myself" was the motto to which this "bulwark of Shakerism," in his sixty-two years as a member of the order, faithfully tried to adhere.

XV

THE INTIMATE BOND

LETTERS FROM SHAKER FRIENDS

Separation from the world was one of the most stringent orders in the early Shaker society. But as time went on the leaders realized that for various reasons, chiefly economic, the Believers could not isolate themselves completely, though they did try, in *The Millennial Laws,* to limit "intercourse with the world" to essentials.

In that effort they were not wholly successful. To all strangers with a friendly or serious interest they were habitually cordial, though reserved. Never did they close their doors or their hearts to the poor and needy. Even within the society, once conjugal love had been abandoned and family ties severed, the law of compensation worked to enhance the affection of brother for sister, and sister for brother. Members greeted each other with the words, "More love, sister," or "More love, brother."

Hunger for friendship and understanding—from the world and within the order—could not, however, be permanently controlled, and we find, in many an account by travelers, an almost pathetic warmth of feeling for the worldly guests. The urge to extend affection beyond boundaries was certainly one of the factors in the weakening of communal solidarity.

Be that as it may, our own experience has demonstrated basically how human relationships may be between these sequestered folk and the world outside. As an English visitor once pointed out, the opinion of persons who may think of the Shakers, as she herself once did, as "either hypocrites or ignorant fanatics," would be "very much raised by a more intimate acquaintance with them." Once the Believers were convinced of the good will of the stranger, welcome was warm and understanding reciprocal. Letters we have received from time to time from our Shaker friends are abundant evidence that Shaker goodness was not confined.

One of our earliest correspondents was Eldress Prudence A. Stickney, successor to Elder Otis Sawyer as head of the Sabbathday

Lake, Maine, society. Her first letter is dated 1929; her last, not long before she died, in 1937. On September 17, 1932, she wrote as follows:

> I am so thankful we have such loyal friends in you, who defend our cause, for you know and understand our homes and lives as few do . . . We do intend to live to the best there is in us, and never let our banners trail in the dust. . . . You seem more like Shakers, than many who have worn the garb, and made outward profession. There was such a pure, elevating influence in your home that we all realized. We all loved you from the first, but love you more now, since we have been in your dear home . . . Always your staunch friend.

In 1937, after the publication of *Shaker Furniture,* came this note:

> My lovely friends: Your wonderful book came Thursday, and how I appreciate the long hours you have put into it, you will never know. Oh, it is all so beautifully done, and expressed, and shows your love and appreciation for what believers have, and are doing, and their religious life. . . .

Eldress Prudence filled her letters not only with news about the weather, the crops, her trips to the Rangeley Lakes and other places selling fancy work, etc., but with her inmost thoughts, her concerns about family affairs, her failing eyesight, her great love of home. She wrote in one of her last letters:

> This is a glorious morning, full of the beauty and goodness of God. How much we have to thank Him for. I love every inch of this sacred hallowed spot, every rock, every blade of grass, and the beautiful trees, whose arms reach up to heaven in their silent benediction, and thanksgiving to God. What a grand world He has given us to use, and not abuse. . . . Now keep well. With much love, I am your sincere friend and Sister.

The "lead" at Canterbury, New Hampshire, at the time of our first visits, was composed of Eldress Josephine E. Wilson and Elder Arthur Bruce, both of whom came to respect and cooperate with our work. Characteristic was the spirit expressed in a letter we had from Eldress Josephine on April 28, 1930:

> We shall be happy to have you stay with us overnight. You have not stayed long enough at one time to call it a visit, nor get acquainted. We have your things you left behind in safe storage . . . You say 'It is kind of us to bother with you!' Now look the word bother up in Webster's Dictionary, *and see* if the definition applies to *friends. Pother* means *to make a stir.* . . . better use this next time, for I will grant you do this, but are not guilty of being a *Bother.* . . .

Elder Arthur was a businesslike but always friendly correspondent, careful to acknowledge the receipt of books and ever ready to write letters of reference. Once, with his associate, Brother Irving, he drove to our home in Pittsfield to deliver in person a roll of Shaker

THE UNITED SOCIETY OF SHAKERS
—FOUNDED 1787—

SADIE A. NEALE
SHAKER FANCY GOODS

Mount Lebanon, New York, June 19ᵗʰ 1932

Dear Mrs. Andrews:

I have the pedals and lams for your loom ready for you, but the pulleys are still in the back ground. I have not found a perfect set as yet.

Better not count on my going to Williamstown to see the loom maker.

Have spent so much time in company with the beautiful of late am losing ground with the useful. Found the two names you requested in our record of deaths. No special history of them. Come and see me at your pleasure.

Sincerely
Sadie A. Neale

THE UNITED SOCIETY OF SHAKERS
—FOUNDED 1787—

SADIE A. NEALE
SHAKER FANCY GOODS

Mount Lebanon, New York, June 27ᵗʰ 1932

Friend Andrews:

For some time I have been meandering around the fields of the past in search of buried treasures; incidentally I came across the names of two characters whom you wanted to hear from. Every material thing has its birth, growth and decay. I do not know anything of the growth of these characters, so am sending only their birth and decay. Noah Osborne = born 1766 = died 1813. Asa Talcott = born 1770 = died Nov. 21 = 1823. This information limited is the best I can give. Kindly remember me to Mrs. Andrews.

Cordially Yours
S. A. Neale

Shaker Village, Sabbathday Lake, Maine, Sept. 17ᵗʰ 1932.

My Very Dear Friends:-

Your letter was very welcome, also price which I am returning in this. We all pronounce it fine, and right to the point. I am so thankful we have such loyal friends in you, who defend our cause, for you know and understand our homes and lives as few do. but I do feel we are better known then we used to be. and people love and respect our work more and more. We do intend to live to the best there is in us, and never let our banners trail in the dust. but keep them to the high inspirational drawings and paintings, not, alas, for us to keep, but to document at our leisure—a gesture, certainly, of confidence. He congratulated us cordially on our first Shaker studies and "the excellent work it emphasizes," assuring us of his "continued regard." And whenever we paid a visit to the village he took pride in seeing personally that we had a sumptuous repast.

With the exception of Walter Shepherd, of the North family in New Lebanon, Elder Arthur was the only "leading brother" we were privileged to know. Elder Walter was more reserved but equally considerate and kind. Once, in answer to a query, he concluded a letter (March 7, 1931) by saying:

> Appreciating your sincere and very friendly interest in the past work of our Society, we know that anything you may write with regard to us will be judicious and friendly.

As a token of such appreciation he consented, on the occasion of an exhibit at the Berkshire Museum, to attend and give an informal talk on the life and work of the Shaker order.

Here again we must acknowledge our debt to Sister Alice Smith at Hancock. We saw more of her than anyone but Sadie, partly because Hancock was nearer our home, partly because she needed contact with people with understanding of her personal problems and aspirations, partly—we admit—because through her assistance many treasures were made available to us, but chiefly because what was at first a casual acquaintance ripened into a rare intimacy. Alice was loyal to Shaker ideals, but she was also realistic, informed as to the idiosyncracies of various members of the society, the opportunities and pitfalls in collecting, and the impact of materialistic pressures on the Shaker spirit. Thus, when one family in New York was threatened by the invasion of commercial interests, "with a large bank roll," she wrote (March 3, 1933):

> Now I am going to be a regular 'watch dog' and hope nothing escapes me—and I can often *guess* as well as 'reckon'—so here's good luck to you—and thank you for all your good work and sincere interest. 'I am with you in the furnace heat,' as the old song goes. Of the earth earthy, Sincerely, Alice.

Further evidence of confidence is furnished by a Watervliet sister, Lucy Bowers, whom we knew only slightly, but who had apparently followed with interest our Shaker activities. Sister Lucy had lived for twenty-eight years at the North family in New Lebanon, from which community she had been transferred to care for an elderly sister at Niskeyuna. On January 14, 1934, she confided to us a secret hope:

> Dear Dr. Andrews. It is with feelings of delicacy that I write to you concerning a little matter that to me is of some importance.
> . . . I have a collection of original writings, essays, pieces of verse, acrostics and sonnets which have been quite neatly copied into

books. . . This work was done between the years 1868 and 1890 while I lived in Lebanon. . . . I pray you will not think me presumptuous if I ask you, whether, in your opinion, there is any way of disposing of them beside burning. My life on earth will take me only a little way into the future, they will not be mine for long. . . . I call them 'The Writings of a Shaker Abecedarian.' Having no educational background, in themselves they are not valuable, but I do not know of any similar Shaker reminiscence. . .

In accepting these fugitive writings, now in our library, we had in mind Sister Lucy's earnest desire that we do what we could to perpetuate the "memoiries" of the Believers.

The final letter to be quoted was from Anna Case, the saintly eldress who was the last leader at Watervliet, the birth place of the American Shakers. Only for a brief period did we know her; she was soon to pass away, and with her a community as old as the republic itself. But we treasure the experience, and the two letters we had from her shaking pen. One of them, undated, reads as follows:

Do please thank Mr. Andrews for His Book. I have passed it on to Str. Lucy [Bowers] who is interested and we shall all have the privilege of reading it. Shakers certainly appreciate it it must have taken time and labor. . . . I am glad that Eldress Fannie (Estabrook) has such a good friend in you. I expect you will discover I cant half see. I've past 90. . . . My sheets is filling, so I'll close by sending choisest Love to Mr. Andrews and Faith Andrews—pretty name. God keep and Bless You. . . . Anna Case.

XVI

COLLECTING PRINTS

Though fine photographs and paintings have been made of Shaker buildings and furniture, there is something about an old print, be it a woodcut, engraving or just a line drawing, which expresses best the simple, forthright Shaker spirit. Adding zest to the search is the fact that very few graphic artists recorded the subject. Of those who worked during the nineteenth century, only five are known by name.

The earliest was Anthony Imbert, who, about 1830, did a lithograph, delicately colored, of the Shaker religious dance. A marine artist by training, Imbert is said to have been the proprietor of the first lithographic establishment in New York City. In 1825, the year in which he illustrated Colden's book on the Erie Canal, he was listed as a "painter" working at 146 Fulton Street. At one time he lived at 79 Murray Street, but by 1831, which was shortly before his death, he had moved to 104 Broadway. His published work included a set of views of the city drawn by A.J. Davis.

The title of our Imbert print is *Shakers—near Lebanon.* It is undated, but was published at 104 Broadway, near Pine Street. The use of the word *Lebanon* instead of the correct "New Lebanon" suggests that it was the peculiarity of the dance in this case the "square order shuffle"—rather than the historical value of the scene which governed the choice of subject. At the time it was probably not a popular subject, or perhaps the edition was a small one. At any rate, our print is the only one we have seen. It is much rarer and finer than the pirated copies, the crude caricatures later made by Kellogg, N. Currier and others.

Kellogg and Currier were not the only ones to render the subject satirically. To make fun of the Shakers, particularly their mode of worship and the doctrine of celibacy, was for a long time the prevalent attitude of the world. Typical of the viewpoint was Thomas Worth's colored lithograph of "The Dance of the Shaker on Sunday," which appeared in the June, 1883, issue of *The Judge.* Another misrepresentation is the sketch, by an anonymous artist, illustrating Artemus Ward's

SHAKERS near LEBANON state of N YORK.
their mode of Worship.   *Drawn from Life.*

Print by Anthony Imbert

essay on the Shakers, one which depicts an elder fondling two young Shaker girls.* Though the humorist thought their religion was "small pertaters," he nevertheless respected their honest dealings and fine craftsmanship. The people were "neat and tidy," he admitted in a lecture: "Your lands is flowin with milk and honey. Your brooms is fine and your apple sass is honest. When a man buys a keg of apple sass of you he don't find a grate many shavins under a few layers of sass—a little Game I'm sorry to say sum of my New Englan ancesters used to practiss. Your garding seeds is fine, and if I should sow 'em on the rock of Gibralter probly I should raise a good mess of garding sass. . ."

After Imbert came John Warner Barber, an artist-chronicler who wandered through New York and New England sketching scenes of towns and points of interest. Barber's *Historical Collections* on Massachusetts, which includes the *Shaker Village in Hancock,* was published in 1839, and the work on New York, with its stark *Shaker*

---

* The drawing bears the initials HLS and in another corner the name Wevill. *The Complete Works of Artemus Ward.* New York, 1887.

Buildings in New Lebanon, in 1841. Outside of their intrinsic charm, each of these pictures—engravings from drawings "taken on the spot"—has historic value, the first because it records the Hancock meeting house and the round stone barn in their original aspect, and the second because it shows the first unitary dwelling of the Church family before it was destroyed by fire. Each catches the spirit of the austerely plain but orderly Shaker scene.

Next, chronologically, is the obscure artist who illustrated a little book entitled *Two Years' Experience Among the Shakers*, published in West Boylston, Massachusetts in 1848 by David R. Lamson, an apostate of the society. Two of the illustrations, "The Whirling Gift" and "The Gift of Father and Son," seem on first sight to be rather inept statements. But when they are enlarged, as the first one was for the original dust jacket of our history of *The People Called Shakers*, it is surprising how much more graphic it became. Doubtlessly Lamson wanted to caricature Shaker rituals, but whoever did the drawings gave them a zestful character. In contrast the third illustration, "The Mountain Meeting," which serves as the frontispiece for the Lamson book, is a stylized rendition, gravely formal, almost abstract in quality, anything but satire.

No artist knew the Shakers so well as Benson John Lossing. At the New Lebanon community, which he visited in the 1850's, he had long talks with the Shaker herbalist, Edward Fowler, and in the course of his stay sketched the medicinal herb shop, various implements used in the herb industry, buildings, costume and other aspects of the culture, recording a way of life for which he had developed a deep interest. The drawings were engraved and published with an unsigned article (by Lossing) in *Harper's New Monthly Magazine* in 1857.

Benson Lossing (1813-1891) was born at Beekman, Dutchess County, New York, the son of John and Miriam (Dorland) Lossing. At twenty-two he became joint editor and proprietor of the *Poughkeepsie Telegraph*, and later one of the editors of a literary fortnightly called the *Poughkeepsie Casket*. In the latter capacity he learned the art of engraving on wood from one J.A. Adams, who did the illustrations for that periodical. In 1833 he married Alice Barritt. Presumably it was with her father, Thomas Barritt, that he subsequently formed the engraving firm of Lossing-Barritt. Moving to New York in 1838, he was occupied in editing and illustrating the weekly *Family Magazine*, writing an *Outline History of the Fine Arts* (1840), and later, among a number of works, his best known ones, the *Pictorial Field Book of the Revolution* (1850-52), and *A Memorial of Alexander Anderson, M.D., the First Engraver on Wood in America* (1872).

Through his daughter, Mrs. Helen Lossing Johnson of Yonkers, N.Y. we obtained one of the artist's finest original sketches, a

The Whirling Gift

Mountain Meeting

Solemn March, The Final Procession

Singing Meeting

Interior of the Meeting-House

Shakers Going to Meeting

watercolor of the "Interior of the Meeting-House," showing a Shaker brother meditating on a bench in the spacious New Lebanon church, and in the background another brother entering the door. It was most delicately done, depicting, in all truth, the peace and sanctity of a building which was the spiritual heart of the community. Mrs. Johnson also gave us one of her father's unpublished manuscripts, a colorful account of his observations on the herb industry and his conversations with Brother Fowler. (See Chapter III).

The work of another competent artist interested in the Shakers was printed on cheap newsprint by *The London Graphic.* In 1870, A. Boyd Houghton visited America on assignment from the paper to record whatever took his fancy. He was a comparatively obscure artist, though he became better known through his illustrations for *The Arabian Nights* and a memoir by Lawrence Housman (A.E's brother), who eulogized his work. When he returned to England, his sketchbook would hardly have seemed to warrant the expense of the trip, for besides a number of steerage drawings, only one other subject captivated him—the Shakers.

Our knowledge of his Shaker engravings came about circuitously. During an exhibition at the Whitney Museum in New York in 1935, a stranger one day engaged us in conversation. An artist himself, as a side line he clipped and sold illustrations from old magazines and newspapers: a sort of one-man Brown Brothers or Bettman Archives. In his stock, he told us, were the following Houghton reproductions: "Shakers at Meeting. The Religious Dance"; "Shakers at Meeting. The Final Procession"; "Shaker Evans at Home"; "Dinner-time at Mount Lebanon"; "Shakers Going to Meeting"; and "A Shaker Sleighing Party." The engravings vibrate with action, and the characterization is imaginative. No one, with the exception of Joseph Becker, caught so well the spirit of Shaker worship.

Of Becker we have little information. He was a staff artist on *Leslie's Popular Monthly,* and in 1885 did an interesting study of a "Singing Meeting" at one of the communities. It was probably Becker who the same year also did a detailed drawing (unsigned) of a round or ring dance at Niskeyuna which conveys vividly the exaltation of the Shaker worshippers as they swung in concentric circles (wheels within wheels) around a chorus of singers.

Also in 1885 a wholesale and jobbing drug establishment in New York, A.J. White of 54 Warren Street, issued a *Shaker Almanac* entitled "The Joys and Sorrows of a Poor Old Man." The line drawings (unsigned) advertising a certain extract of roots called

Shakeress Pasting the Labels on Bottles Containing the Shaker Extract of Roots, or Seigel's Syrup.

The Shakers in Niskayuna—Enjoying a Sleigh-ride.

"Seigel's Syrup," though printed on cheap pulp, are accurate and charming. Particularly in those cuts showing Shaker sisters cooking, sealing and pasting labels on bottles there is a careful rendition of such details as kerchiefs, net caps, aprons and chairs.

Shaker craftsmanship attracted the attention of two artist-friends, Armin Landeck and Charles Sheeler. In the late 1930's Landeck did an etching of a "Shaker Stove" which is one of our most valued possessions. Through the kindness of Sister Sadie Neale he was permitted to improvise a studio in a disused shop, where he set up a typical wood-burning box stove, complete with stove-board and angled pipe. The print, showing the stove sharply massed against a white plastered wall on which it casts its shadow, is a striking study in pure geometric form.

The clean-lined, spare functionalism of Shaker furniture and architecture had a strong appeal for Charles Sheeler and greatly influenced his art. He collected several fine examples of craftsmanship, and beginning in the 1930's, did a number of drawings and paintings, compositions employing both furniture design and architectural forms. That he was sensitive also to the spirit suffusing these forms, his impressions of the meeting house at New Lebanon bear witness:

> The sense of light and spaciousness received upon entering the hall is indicative of similar spiritual qualities of the Shakers. Instinctively one takes a deep breath, as in the midst of some moving and exalted association with nature. There were no dark corners in those lives. Their religion thrived on light rather than the envelopment of a dark mystery—with the Shakers all was light, in their crafts and equally with their architecture.*

For the first time, in Sheeler's work, color and light were used to transmit the inherent beauty of Shaker craftsmanship. This, for us, was a revelation and a delight.

A CURIO

No likeness of Ann Lee is known. Even the descriptions of her physical appearance vary. But there does exist a "psychometric portrait" which received a certain amount of attention in the society.

The "portrait" was one of the by-products of the pseudo-science of phrenology, a cult which had many devotees in America—including members of the Shaker order—in the years following the Civil War. One was apt to come across, in the family libraries, copies of the

---

* Constance Rourke, *Charles Sheeler, An Artist in the American Tradition.*

illustrated annuals of phrenology and physiognomy; and in our collection is one of the white plaster heads (found in a nurse-shop) with sections of the brain numbered to denote the seats of various mental faculties.

Thumbing through the Annual for 1872 we were surprised to find the portrait in question with a letter from Elder G.A. Lomas, editor of *The Shaker,* to S.R. Wells, editor of the Annual, explaining its origin. Wrote Lomas:

> The picture is a copy from a crayon purported to be psychometrically drawn by one Milleson, of New York. The picture, while in the hands of the artist, was not recognized by him nor by any of his friends. . . . An individual named Trow, also of New York City, took the picture to a test medium or psychological expert, and before presenting the picture, the medium began moving around the room after the marching manner of the Shakers, singing a genuine Shaker song at the same time; at the conclusion of the exercise the medium asserted that the likeness of Ann Lee, mother of the Shakers' faith, was in the possession of the inquirer!*

Lomas thought that *one* of several descriptions of Mother Ann agreed "very uniformly" with the portrait. He did not admire the "lower face," with its pointed chin and the mouth "looking as if capable of scolding." But the "brain-house" (which Wells thought showed "a large amount of reflective and speculative intellect, and an excessive development of the organs of Benevolence, Veneration and Spirituality") was, in Lomas' opinion, "surpassing beautiful." We cannot agree with that opinion. For us the "portrait" of the prophetess is neither appealing nor convincing as a portrait of one who inspired intelligent, devout people to follow her in the footsteps of the Master.

* Letter from the Office of *The Shaker,* Shakers, Albany Co., N.Y. May 9th, 1871. From *The Illustrated Annuals of Phrenology and Physiognomy For the Years 1865-1873,* New York, by S.R. Wells. (Annual for 1872, pp. 38-41.)

XVII

A WOODCUT ARTIST SPEAKS HIS MIND

Though J.J. Lankes never did a finished woodcut on a Shaker theme, we wish that he had, for more than anyone we knew he could capture, in black and white, the subtle moods of New England. His "Road to Bennington" and "Rain in the Berkshires," which now hang on the wall of the barn in which I am writing this rainy day, are deeply evocative expressions of which we never tire. Lankes, a dissenter from the materialism of the day, was captivated by the Shakers' will to excel the world, in conduct as in craftsmanship. His visits to our farm in Richmond were followed by letters in which he contrasted, in his inimitable salty style, the sins of industrialism with the Shaker ideal of rectitude in the work of hands. Once he got as far as to submit proof of a woodcut of an oval box, but the project was never finished.

His comments on that experiment illustrate his humility, the care with which he worked:

> I made a number of mistakes on it. First, the use of a maple veneered block. This would be a technical mistake, and only a woodcutter would realize the statement without an explanation. My idea was to suggest woodiness as much as possible, and by using the same kind of wood as the box, the suggestiveness would be greater. This sounds like carrying notions too far. Well, maple wood is fibrous, which means that the cutting is troublesome because the hairlike fibers have to be removed. You will notice on the proof where some came into evidence. They cross the cut lines at right angles. This cut is not a serious mistake—if a mistake at all except in the matter of consuming time. . . .

Regretting that conditions prevented him from doing an engraving of the round stone barn at Hancock, a subject that particularly interested him, he wrote:

> I can't fight with the circumstance that makes it necessary for me to absorb a scene before I can even draw it. That is an inherent weakness in my character. I've got to mull over a subject quite a while before I can do anything with it.

How deeply this sensitive artist, like the Shakers, deplored the vanities and follies of the world is illustrated in another letter, written during the second World War. He found *The Community Industries of the Shakers,* "fascinating in this day of Progress for Destruction" and wrote:

> The thought that comes uppermost in my mind on reading of the activities of the Shakers is that our Progress has been a sad delusion. Maybe its trend was inevitable, and the result, like any bodily disease, a breaking out of corruption. A pox. I could have been a Shaker, altho I dunno about celibacy. A tool should be used, say I. Maybe it was chastity that broke up the society! Otherwise the Shakers were smart.

Then he let himself go:

> What a God awful mess we are in now—even without the war! Lost souls—sloshing around in materialistic quagmires. Three women can't get together but they go at one of them. The church is but an excuse to scratch the hell out of someone—unfortunate or too individualistic to care a damn for their behavior pattern. And the men—cogs in small wheels in large machines—completely frustrated in all their creative impulses. They can't make even an outhouse now. Lawncutting, golfing, poker, drinking, wenching— the women fashions, teas, bridge, gossip, tin-can opening, complaining. Hell. Hardly one has a purpose in life. . . .
>
> Humanity may come back to Shaker philosophy in essence one of these days—when it's had it's fill of the garbage that passes as Progress.

Of all the rewards of collecting, the collecting of friends and their letters we account the best.

XVIII

COLLECTING MANUSCRIPTS

To the historian seeking new data on any given subject there is nothing more exciting than the discovery of an unpublished manuscript. If the subject be an individual, it may be a journal kept by that person, letters he had written or received, notes which throw additional light on his work. As primary source material, it has basic value. But it is more than that. A manuscript is an intimate projection of the writer's personality. The original writing is to its printed form what an original drawing is to the engraving in a book. The illustrations in Barber, as we have related, are delightful; but when we saw his original sketches, we felt that we were in the presence of the artist himself.

Excitement is compounded when the writings record the thought and experience not only of one person but of a whole people. The Shakers were an expressive folk. They cared so much about the cause to which they had committed themselves that—even if their laws had not encouraged the keeping of records—they would have kept journals of their own and the society's affairs. As it was, their gospel statutes enjoined the practice as one promoting order and use and "increasing the work." Scribes were appointed to preserve accounts of meetings and communications from the spiritual world; hymns and dance songs were "pricked for the purpose of retaining them"; copies of official letters were required; and in both the sisters' and brethren's departments, daybooks, ledgers and journals were faithfully kept for the enlightenment of the trustees and ministry.

We were fortunate in that much of our research centered in the Church family at New Lebanon, which was the seat of the central ministry, the largest family in the largest community, and the chief repository of records. During the years of our most active collecting this family was in the process of liquidation. The opportunity existed, therefore, to acquire a mass of material which had been neglected or forgotten. There were Shakers still living, however, in New Lebanon, Hancock and other societies, who sensed the historical value of such papers and who, honoring our motives, entrusted them to our care. Some of our most precious manuscripts, such as the original covenant of 1795, came to us by personal gift.

Others were found in out of the way places. A cupboard in the trustees' office at New Lebanon held bundles of old papers: deeds, indentures, "discharges," wills, memoranda, letters—many going back to the beginning of the movement. In attics, shops and stores we found scores of business records: daybooks, "poor office" accounts, vital statistics, "minute books," records by seedsmen and herbalists, journals on farming, tanning, weaving, dyeing, tailoring, bonnet making, basketry, bee-keeping, chair manufacture, nursing and so on. In a built-in cupboard at Hancock were originals or copies of the letters written to the elders there by leaders in the Ohio and Kentucky societies, the earliest ones dating from 1805. Tucked away in a chest drawer in an anteroom of a New Lebanon dwelling was Isaac Youngs' "Concise View," a detailed history of the movement up to 1857; and in another chest Benjamin Seth Youngs' "Journal of One Year" (1805), in which he recounted the experiences of the three eastern missionaries in opening the gospel in Ohio and Kentucky. Here also was "Little Benjamin's" journal of his mission to the Shawnee Indians in 1805. Another find was a "transcriber's" copy of the fascinating "Sketch of the Life and Experience of Issachar Bates," one of Benjamin's fellow missionaries from New Lebanon. (The "Sketch" is fully described later in this chapter.)

When one has been working in a chosen field for years one gets to know pretty well those actors who played leading roles, in this case the aforementioned "witnesses," such contemporaries as Mother Lucy Wright and Seth Wells, and later such leaders as Bishop Hervey Eads and Frederick Evans. And having known them in books and pamphlets, one comes across their handwriting with an awakened sense of their reality as participants in the drama. The cross which Ann Lee placed beside her name on her banns of marriage was just "her mark," but evidence, nevertheless, that she lived, with hope of happiness. The will of David Darrow, the "father" of Shakerism in the West, is a testament of consecration, a worthy memorial to a man who gave up all he possessed to follow Christ. How satisfying it was to find the documents, written and signed by Seth Youngs Wells, the organizer and first superintendent of Shaker schools, "On Learning and the Use of Books," and "On the Importance of Keeping Correct Book Accounts," or to find on the fly leaf of a presentation copy of *The Kentucky Revival* the name of the author, the scholarly Richard McNemar.

Of the seven Shakers who emigrated from England in 1774 seeking religious freedom in a new land, we have manuscripts by two.

One is a small document recording a business transaction signed by James Shepherd, who was one of the witnesses at the marriage of Mother Ann to Abraham Standerin. The other is a letter (found with a number of miscellaneous papers in a box at Hancock) written in 1787 from Ashfield, Massachusetts by Father James Whittaker, Mother Ann's successor as leader of the society, to Josiah Talcott, a Hancock farmer. In it Ann's youthful disciple urges Josiah, a prospective convert, to get his farm in readiness, "for you have land enough," he wrote, "to maintain three families or more, well improved."*

One of the most valuable manuscripts which came to light in our search and research was *The Millennial Laws* of the Shakers, which were "established" in the Church by Father Joseph Meacham and Mother Lucy Wright and their successors. Recorded at New Lebanon in 1821 and revised in 1845, these statutes and ordinances constituted the by-laws of the sect. Though they include all the orders governing organization and practice they were never printed, and it came as a surprise to us that such a compilation existed. To find them, in several neatly written copies, was an exciting discovery, for they were a most important contribution to our knowledge of Shaker communitarianism.

SKETCH OF THE LIFE AND EXPERIENCE OF ISSACHAR BATES, SEN.

The Shaker movement received initial impetus from the spirit of revivalism, and missions into parts of New York and New England resulted in hundreds of conversions. So when news of another great "awakening" in Kentucky and Ohio reached the central ministry they decided to proselytize again, sending three of their most competent preachers to that frontier country. One of them, Issachar Bates, Sen. was a unique personality, and the "Sketch" is one of the most readable documents in the annals of the society. His lively narrative must have been popular within the order itself, for several copies of the manuscript exist, though it was never published in its entirety.

Bates had a great zest for living. He loved to play on his fife, to sing popular songs, and to compose—poems, songs, and memoirs. When he was 76 years old (in 1834) he wrote with satisfaction that his room was furnished with "plenty of writing-paper of the best kind—and what doth hinder me from writing as much as I am able"—adding whimsically, "And if some of it should be chaffy, there is generally wind enough to blow it off."

Four passages from the "Sketch" are selected not only to give the

---

* The letter is quoted in full in *The Shaker Shaken,* (New Haven, 1934), a booklet printed at the Bibliographical Press by students of our friend Carl Purington Rollins, printer to Yale University.

flavor of his style, his sense of humor, etc., but because these excerpts illuminate certain aspects of the Shaker theme: (1) reasons why men of character and conscience joined the sect; (2) some of the hardships encountered in promulgating its peculiar doctrine; (3) the care of the aged; and (4) the importance placed by the Shakers, as well as the Essenes, on the virtue of silence.

(1)

Issachar was born in the town of Hingham, Massachusetts, on January 29, 1758, of pious Presbyterian parents. Though he was a normal "mischievous" boy, he thought much about God, believing that He was "all holy, righteous and good, and I must be so too, or never see His face in peace." He kept the Sabbath strictly, and learned the "little praises, cradle hymns, catechisms, prayers, creeds, etc." Yet he was afraid "that God would come upon me, some day in judgement, because I was not good." He used to watch the heavens for "signs and wonders."

A few years before the Revolution, when Issachar was eleven years old, he saw the first of these signs, the "northern lights. . . night after night, for weeks," and then others: once a "blazing comet . . . bell-muzzled, in perfect shape of a trumpet . . . some nights as red as blood," and later what appeared to be a "black vane, about the size of a common stove pipe . . . about five rods long, and crooked like a black snake, and in the same shape, tapering at both ends . . . It began to gather up like a horse-leach, and gathered into a round ball, about the size of an eighteen inch bomb shell, and then exploded. The fire flew in every direction, and the report was as loud as any cannon I ever heard only not so sharp; and in one moment the sky was as red as blood!"

Such phenomena—warnings, people thought, of an impending day of judgment—created "doleful feelings" in the sensitive boy's mind, and though a Deist, in talking about them, derided the signs and "took off a part of the sharp edge" of his anxiety, he still "kept a sharp lookout."

The "Sketch" continues with an account of Issachar's experiences in the war, in which he served as a fifer and fife major, and where, in the battles of Bunker Hill and other engagements he saw what he felt was the literal fulfillment of his visions. During the war he married one Lovina Maynard, by whom he had eleven children. After the war he bought a small farm, but as he could not get rich fast enough at that, he went to "speculating in goods, horses, cattle, sheep, hogs and everything else that a fool could take a notion to."

During these years of varied business ventures, Issachar was full of serious thoughts, but "always hated conviction." Then one morning, when he was 37 years of age, as he opened the door to go to work, and cast his eyes on his children, he determined to begin to mend his life: he had "a clear view of God, that he was all fitness, and I was just the reverse." Disturbed by his past sins and imperfections, he resolved "to come to an honest settlement with God if possible."

But the way was hard and obscure. He joined the Baptist church, and though he rejected its creed of election, perseverance and original sin as "damning to every creature," he was later baptized and became a lay preacher. Still he was unsatisfied. "Notions of flesh began to return, which felt more deathly to me than the bite of a rattlesnake." Consciousness of past sins oppressed him: "the works of the flesh, bearing arms, swearing oaths, dressing in the fashions of the world, etc."

Sometimes, however, in search of the way to reconciliation, he had moments of release:

> Going home one evening with the sore still in my breast, or rather in my heart, and in tormenting pain . . . right there in the middle of the road, in a moment, in the twinkling of an eye, a hot flash like lightning struck me thro' the neck and shoulders into my heart, and drove out the sore lump, and every weight about me, and left me feeling as light as nothing, with my hands stretched up, and on my tiptoes, expecting every step, to leave the earth and step into the air. Here I had the perfect knowledge of joy unspeakable and full of glory . . . . Then I passed by . . . . a burying yard, (the sight of which had always filled me with dread,) and stretched out my hand over the fence, and bid defiance to the grave, to death, and to hell. And I have never been afraid of that Monster . . . . from that time henceforth, even forever. . .

Nevertheless it was not till Issachar heard of the Shakers—"the only people who did not live after the flesh"—that he put the "world"—his wife, his children, his earthly possessions—behind him. Since childhood he had never been able to forget Ezekiel's prophecy of the end of the world. The wrath of God was a terrible reality. But the Shakers, he heard, in separating from "the course of this world," had already entered the resurrection life, and had made their peace with the Creator.

So one day, on the pretext of visiting some relatives, he left home for the community at New Lebanon, where he talked with Ebenezer Cooley, the elder of the novitiate family. "My whole stay at Lebanon was not much over an hour," he recalled, "for we did business quick. I ate quick and talked quick, heard quick and started back home quick, for I was quickened." Returning soon afterwards, he confessed his sins and joined the order where he was to spend the rest of his days.

(2)

June, 1808, found Issachar and other members of a Shaker mission at a place called Busroe Creek on the Wabash, in Indiana Territory, where "a people had been waiting" to hear the Word. Though Governor Harrison had assured them that under the laws of the United States they had a right to preach their faith, that anyone had a right to embrace it, and that the mission would be protected, the Shakers encountered opposition on several occasions. The second time that Bates visited Busroe, accompanied by Malcolm Worley and Matthew Houston, a "mob of 42," led by one John Thompson, came upon them on horseback, with ropes to bind them. Thompson stepped up to him, Issachar relates, and shouted:

"Come, prepare yourself to move."

"Move where," said I.

"Out of this country," said he, "for you have ruinted (sic) a fine neighborhood, and now we intend to fix you. Your hats are too big, we shall have a part of them off, and your coats are too large, we shall have a part of them off. And seeing you will have nothing to do with women, we will fix you so that you will not be able to perform."

"Well," said I, "have you any precept?"

"Yes, precept enough for you."

"Well, you must show it."

"D—D you, get on your horses, for you shall go."

"Well, I will tell you up and down, we shall not go with a mob."

Then John Hadden spoke, "If *you* don't go and get your horses, *I* will get them, *for you shall go,* so where are they?"

"They are in William Berry's stable. But if you get them, we shall not go onto them."

"Well then, we will put you on."

"Well, then, we will get off again."

"Well, then, we will tie you on."

"Well you will have a hard job of it before you get thro."

But by this time all the rest of the mob were laughin, and said, "Come let us go."

Further on in the manuscript Bates summarizes his experience in traveling from Union Village, the headquarters of Shakerism in the West, to this "Wabash world":

How many times have I plunged thro' that doleful trace 240 miles, and 150 of it without a cabin: and the most difficult water that ever ran above ground. And one time in particular, when Elder Benjamin, Richard McNemar and myself started the 16th of January 1809 with five days provision, and had to live on that 16 days freezing and starving thro' seas of ice and water, climing old trees that were afloat, riding old logs across deep waters, and many other projects to get along at all, and in which journey I froze both of my great toe nails out by the roots, and Richard and I called to mind a journey we took to Greenville to see the Shawnee Indians

when we had to swim Kethwatha River twice with our persecutors
at our heels. . . .

(3)

The consideration shown by the Shakers to the aged and infirm
is illustrated in a letter which Issachar wrote in January, 1834, from
his home in Watervliet, Ohio, to friends in the South Union colony in
southern Kentucky. He was then seventy-six years old, and had been
"quite weakly with a palpitation of the heart, inflamation and swelling
of the bowels, cold feet and legs." He writes, "I will simply tell you how
I have been treated through my weakness," asking to be excused if he
were "a little silly" in his old age:

> Well this is a handsome room with two light windows, with
> nice window blinds, a good little stove and fireplace—a good husk
> bed with the best of bedding—a bureau with four drawers in it—
> a table—a woodbox—a looking glass—a comb case—the little
> spotted trunk you know, Father David's great chair, and three
> others besides. Spit box—fire shovel and tongs—blow-pipe and
> matches—brooms and brushes—pipes and tobacco, and money to
> buy more with. Candle, candlestick and snuffers—pitcher and
> wash bowl, chip-basket and bed-mug—razor—lather box and
> soap, and a number more useful and pretty things. A nice little
> clock, that keeps very good time, and Eldress Molly's pretty little
> Peacock's tail hanging up in sight, and as many books as I wish
> to read—and pen and ink, and you know that I have a plenty of
> writing-paper of the best kind. . .
>
> I must tell you how I am waited on. Elder Eleazer is my attor-
> ney at law—Brother Robert visits me as he can get time. Thomas
> Williams provides my wood and does it completely. Martial Pat-
> terson sleeps in the room with me and attends to my wants. Eldress
> Salome makes my bed and cleans my room. Sister Eunice cooks
> for me—Jenny Patterson is my nurse, and is very attentive and
> kind, and feeds me all the nasty bitter stuff that can be thought
> of. . . .

(4)

"World's people" who visited the communal homes of the Shakers
during the last century were invariably impressed by their cleanliness,
order and quietude. "You feel that you are beyond the realm of hurry,"
wrote one of these visitors, "there is no restlessness, or fret of business,
or anxiety about anything; it is as if the work was done, and it was one
eternal afternoon."

To preserve such peace and calm, however, in homes occupied
sometimes by as many as a hundred or more brethren and sisters, it
was necessary to exercise authority and constant care. As attestation
we select the testimony on "unnecessary noise" which Issachar delivered to the Watervliet family on his seventy-sixth birthday:

As I had a privilege a few evenings past of opening my mind in meeting, by way of thanksgiving, complaint and request, in relation to unnecessary noise in the house—, yet I cannot feel satisfied to drop the subject here, but wish to show the necessary causes from which these noises may be and still are multiplied, which are as follows:

Now in this building, (house and kitchen,) there are fifty-eight doors for the convenience of the different appartments. The doors are passed and repassed through more than two thousand times a day,—opened and shut either by those that have some fear and care, with softness, or by those that have neither fear nor care with a bang like a little sharp clap of thunder.

Now these noise makers are so accustomed to making a noise: —they are not a judge of noise—they cannot even distinguish between a big noise and a little one, no more than a man in the woods in the time of a hurricane can distinguish which tree makes the loudest noise by falling—for with him it is all one noise.

There are twenty three fires kept in this building which will require, at least, two armfuls of wood a day for each fire. Here are forty six armfuls of wood to be brought into this house in a day, either put carefully into a woodbox, or thrown without care or feeling into the box or on the floor, and make as many claps of wooden thunder as there are armfuls of wood, every one jarring the whole house. Each of these fires must be recruited, at least, five times a day. These wood boxes must be visited one hundred and fifteen times in a day, either to take out the wood carefully, or else to ransack and rustle the whole pile, till the house is filled with the racket.

Now add to this the countless variety of noises that happen every day, such as moving chairs, benches, tables, pots, kettles, buckets, tubs, and hundreds of other things, some necessary and some unnecessary. Last of all add to the music, more than forty thousand steps in a day of brethren and sisters across the floors, some with a little softness and care, others like horses on the barn floor in fly time.

Now amidst all this variety of noises who is able to tell how long a time of cessation of noise there will be, from four o'clock in the morning, till eleven in the evening.

And after all this, supposing that all of us, or a part of us should set up our wills that we are not going to learn anything further in these notions, but mean to step as we please, and shut doors as we please, and this sense should prevail, in so large a family as this, and it must be so, I can say for one, in solemn fear, I should desire but one more additional noise to make a complete bedlam, and that would be a drum to beat the long roll continually, to drown and confound those unnecessary, unreasonable, uneternal, unusual, unchristian and ungodly noises, and as far as possible to consolidate them in one horrid sound of confusion.

But as one of old said, "Beloved, we are persuaded better things of you tho' we thus speak." And I want you to know that I am not so much averse to noise as you may suppose. I love a necessary noise. I love to hear a grist mill, and a saw mill, and a fulling mill, and all such noises as these. But I hate to hear a fool snapping a whip.

I love to see and hear a beautiful brother or sister stepping across the room with a soft elastic step, and when they come to a door, know that it is a door, and that they have got to go thro' carefully, and when they are thro' turn their face to it and shut it easy. But I hate to see or hear a heavy footed brother or sister thumping across the floor, co-lump, co-lump, co-lump, and when they get to the door not think whether it is a door or a pair of bars, —whether they are going into another room or into a field and when they get thro' turn tail to, and bang it after them, without one thought of what they are about.

Now perhaps some may be offended at me for being so plain and blunt on these matters. But I suppose you know that I don't care for that. And perhaps some may think that it means me.— Well if it does you will please me very much if you will quit it; and if it does not mean you, then you are safe enough. But to take off all occasion of hard feelings, against me, I will set the example, and you may follow me if you please.

I honestly confess before God, and all of you, my brethren and sisters, that it means me, and I solemnly declare that I will quit it. And I will keep the order of the gospel, as it has been taught us from the beginning. I will walk softly, I will be careful in opening and shutting doors, and in everything that I put my hands to. And if everyone in the family will do this, we shall soon feel the glory of God all over the house,—Every door will give glory to God, and every wood box will open its mouth and cry peace, peace and abundance of peace—And every step across the floor will proclaim that Wisdom's ways are ways of pleasantness, and all her paths and all her steps are peace.

Issachar

BROTHER ISAAC NEWTON YOUNGS:
HIS HISTORY IN VERSE

If one would know the values for which the Shakers stood, there is no better measure than the lives of those who gave their all to the cause. Issachar Bates was such a one, Benjamin Youngs, another. A third, whose "history in verse" we are transcribing, was the nephew of Benjamin. We have met him before, as the author of that blue paper-covered treatise on the "Rudiments of Music: for new Beginners," copies of which we found in the schoolhouse attic.

July 4th, 1837.

Forty four years now since my birth,
And I'm still living on the earth,

And full of bus'ness night and day;
With scarce a moments time to play;
I've work enough, that's now on hand
For 15 years, for any man.
I'm overrun with work and chores
Upon the farm or within doors.

Which ever way I turn my eyes;
Enough to fill me with surprise.
How can I bear with such a plan?
No time to be a gentleman!
All work-work-work, still rushing on,
And *conscience* too still pushing on:
When will this working all be done?
When will this lengthy thread be spun?

As long as *working* is the cry.
How can I e'er find time to die?
Must I be sick to get away?
O that is harder yet, I say!
But still at work I won't complain,
Upon the whole I think 'tis gain.
Its' none too bad for any man
To do what little good he can.

Be sure the Devil will have to flee,
And seek some other place but me
To find a workshop to his crook
'Mongst idle brains, or I've mistook
I don't pretend I've done too much,
I don't a single stroke begrutch.
But if I'de time to give a sketch
My gone by years in view to fetch,

'Twould take a deal of ink and paper
And be withall a useless caper!
To trace my crooked road to glory
Would be a very lengthy story.
In childish days, what scenes untold
To my astonished view unfold!
From birth to five or six years old
I know not much but what I'm told.

When under my Aunt Molly's care,
Some dirty scrapes no doubt there were;
But at the age of seven or eight,
Some wond'rous feats I could relate.
My mighty scene (?) of Cat and sled,
(Enough to rack a gen'ral's head!)
My sermon to the wicked Len!
Would make you stare, you may depend.

And then, to push the Capshief higher,
My solemn trial of hell fire!
O the deep views I witness'd then
Can't be portray'd by Mortal's pen!
To read in books I much desir'd,
To skill in clocks I *too* aspir'd.
In making dams and woodmills too,
I often found much work to do.

But this I hastily skip o'er
And pass to the age of ten or more.
My travel in back order times,
Would greatly lengthen out my rhymes;
My mountains scenes, also, alas!
How glad I am those days are past.*
A pleasant dream, I here could tell,
How I, the mountain bade farewell;

*Twas here that I did undertake
A little wooden clock to make,
But Abigail Richardson
Burnt it all up—for her own fun.
A flogging too she undertook
To give to me (by hook or crook,)
And for the same I ran away
And told what had took place that day.
But still I feel a kind regard,
Nor do I wish friend Nabby hard;
But lazy Calvin, (Nabby's son,)
I hold some *aught* 'gainst him I own!

And how to Watervliet I went,
And there 3 years or more I spent.
At Watervliet time swiftly ran,
Here I the taylor's trade began.
And still my head was full of notions
And oft bro't trouble for my portion,
Machines and woodmills seem'd so *nice*
I would get caught in some device.

One time, a woodmill I erected
Soon to be finish'd I expected—
But O! I suffer'd the disgrace
To see it burnt before my face!
How oft I cut some silly caper
Not fit to tell about, on paper!
In plays and childish fooleries,
And many kinds of drolleries!

And *working hard* I hated then,
As bad as now, you may depend;

I oft had spells of eating pouts,
And getting mad, or there abouts!
But after all, I need not lie
To say that some were worse than I!
When near 14—at Lebanon
At length I found a settl'd home.

Where thirty years have roll'd away,
(And what's to come I cannot say)
I've not half time, (it now appears)
To picture out these 30 years
I long was boyish, you might know
Untill I had full time to grow.
When first I came, I felt so well
Just how to act, I could not tell.

But I suppose, upon the whole
To *sober folks,* I acted droll.
Some feats of rat-ship I display'd
Which rais'd my fame, it may be said.
And scenes abundant pass'd away
Of which I've little here to say.
(Wild oats enough no doubt I sow'd
(And left to grow upon the road.

There were a number gather'd in
With whom I felt quite near akin.
Friend Garret Lawrence, (late deceas'd)
Among my mates was not the least,
Much real comfort we have taken,
If I am not a deal mistaken:
We loved to talk and make up rhymes
& have some simple sprees, sometimes.

And others I could mention too,
Whose love was near, & friendship true.
As I grew up to reason's age,
More solemn tho'ts my mind engag'd,
The childish season was exchang'd,
For scenes of manhood, new & strange
New cares arose, new billows roar,
New trails, I knew not before.

Satan oft laid his tempting snare
& cross'd my track, most ev'rywhere;
I pass'd thro' many sober times,
Which I shall not put into rhymes.
Religious things I here might mention
Which claims good part of my attention
The Lord beheld me night and day
The Devil watch'd me for his prey.

And conscience hanging round about me,
All seem'd to try my courage stoutly.
I've been perplex'd all round about,
But still, did never yield to doubt
About the truth of sacred things;
Or what to souls true comfort brings;
And still I hold my courage fast,
The golden prize I'll gain at last.

I've always found enough to do,
Some pleasant times, some grievious too
Of various kinds of work I've had
Enough to make me sour or sad,
Of tayl'ring, Join'ring farming too,
Almost all kinds that are to do,
Blacksmithing, Tinkering, Mason work,
When could I find a time to shurk?

Clock work, Jenny work, keeping school
Enough to puzzle any fool!
An endless list of chores & notions,
To keep me in *perpetual motion*
O who on earth could have invented
Such a picture here presented?
How well applied the saying comes,
"Jack at all trades, good at none!"

And now, lest I get out of work,
Or find a little time to shurk;
I have a call to try my skill
To frame a wood-house if I will.
"So at the work I freely go,"
This day begin to make a show,
And hope within the coming year,
A finish'd wood-house may appear.

And by the time I'm 45
If I should be well, & alive
I hope some better times to see;—
For that is just the way with me,
To always look for better days
With brighter sun, more cheering rays
Yet ne'er to slight my pleasant bliss,
Nor present happiness to miss;—

But Make the best of everything,
And let each day its fortune bring.
And should I live to 85,
I hope to be awake—alive
And when I close my days on earth
Straight forward I'll proceed in mirth

And bless the Lord, while ages roll,
Who gave to me a living soul.

Amen, amen, so let it be—
And here I'll cut short you see.—

At twelve o'clock one night when he had finished his "rhymes," Isaac added this "apology":

When I began my airy song,
I did not think of being long;
But when I got right well agoing,
Just where to stop, there was no knowing!

But if to read it, wearies you,
You need not read it wholy thro';
(Lest it should irritate your lungs.)
My name is called Isaac Youngs

OTHER MANUSCRIPTS

Besides those from prominent members, many manuscripts that were anonymous came into our hands over the years. Often they were rhymes in a humorous vein, touching on particular events but more frequently on common concerns in the daily life of the order. "A Robber Hymn," composed at Union Village, Ohio, and sung the day after the event, tells how a chair from the attic struck the head of one of a band of robbers, causing them to flee as from some supernatural agency. Typical of the Shaker habit of investing material objects with human qualities is the poem "Shaker Door," in which the door, having kept out the snow and rain, heat and cold for 40 years, complains that though it was "a true non-resistant" its patience was wearing out:

The tall and the short, weak and strong
All feel it was their duty, as they pass along
To slam me and bang me, as hard as they can
As tho' I had injured the whole race of man.

In "An Epilogue of the Old Bench," the bench unburdens its grief at being removed, after 29 years of service, from the kitchen among "those who were clean," to a shop where it was used for "picking chickens," and finally to the woodpile:

"I thought 'twas in usefulness that we all found
A lasting repose on Cannan's fair ground
And now that I'm old and rather decrepit
To put on more burden does seem to me wicked. . . ."
Its end was in sight, with "splittings and sawings":
"But as 'tis my motto my will to resign
Should I burn at the stake I will not repine."

In a similar catagory is "A Concise Description of a Spiritual Loom. In which we are daily weaving a *Garment of Righteousness.*" composed by Sister Amelia Calver of New Lebanon "when quite young." Every one of the 34 parts of the loom represented a given virtue: faith, conviction, confession, purity, humility, order, the cross, and so on.

A Concise Description of a Spiritual Loom. In which we are daily weaving
A GARMENT OF RIGHTEOUSNESS

1st.   *The Frame*   *Virtue*
The *Frame* is our whole deportment, and it should consist of *Virtue.*

2nd.   *Warp*   *Faith*
The *Warp* is the foundation of our garment, which must be good *Faith.*

3rd.   *Filling*   *Works of Faith*
It is our *Works* that form the *Filling* of our garment.

4th.   *Cloth Beam Rod*   *Prayer*
If we are virtuous we shall resort to *Prayer,* and the *Cloth Beam Rod* is the next thing in a loom towards weaving.

5th.   *Cloth Rod Pins*   *Firmness*
Unless we have *Firmness* and earnestness in our prayers they are not of much value neither is the rod useful unless held by these *Pins.*

6th.   *Cloth Cord*   *Conviction*
The light of *Conviction* is then opened into our souls which is the *Cord* to fasten our prayers and our next duty together.

7th.   *Cloth Rod*   *Confession of Sin*
Our next duty is to *right our wrongs.* This forms a *Rod,* the foundation for us to fasten our faith to, to commence weaving.

8th.   *Yarn Rods*   *Honesty*
We must have *Honesty* to keep our Warp straight and open; which are the *Yarn Rods.*

9th.   *Cloth Beam*   *Hope*
After we have become convicted and have honestly done our first duty, then we can Hope for better things, as we form our garment we therefore wind it on the *Hope* or *Cloth Beam.*

10th.   *Quill*   *Conscience*
But without a *Conscience* whose dictates we act from our garment is not woven. This is the *Quill* from which our Filling proceeds.

11th.   *Shuttle*   *Purity*
We must also keep our Conscience steadfast in *Purity* as the Quill is in the *Shuttle.*

12th.   *Lathe*   *Truth*
Truth serves to form our garment solid as does the *Lathe.*

13th.   *Comb*   *Sincerity*
The Lathe rests on the *Comb* as Truth does on *Sincerity.*

14th.   *Harness*   *Tribulation*
Mother Ann said "no soul can travel one step in the way of God only thro' *Tribulation.*" And all our Warp or Faith must go thro' the *Harness,* (that is being well tried) before it is woven.

15th.   *Reed*   *Order*
The *Reed* keeps the Thread in their proper rectitude as does *Order.*

16th.   *Rod Beam*   *Courage*
The *Rod Beam* holds up the yarn, so *Courage* holds Faith in its duty.

17th.   *Tramp*   *Obedience*
The *Tramp* winds up the Cloth after it is woven as we in *Obedience* secure our garment.

18th.   *Large Catch*   *The Cross*
The *Large Catch* is the *Cross* at which we grasp & take up, in so doing we get more Faith in the gospel to form our garment of.

19th.   *Treadles*   *Perseverance*
But unless we have *Treadles* we cannot weave neither can we increase any in our spiritual work without *Perseverance.*

20th.   *Spring Shafts*   *Wisdom*
The *Spring Shafts* direct the Treadles as *Wisdom* does Perseverance.

21st.   *Treadle Straps*   *Forbearance*
The *Treadle Straps* hold the Shafts, Treadles & Harness together & *Forbearance* must hold us to tribulation etc.

22nd.   *Treadle Pins*   *Humility*
If we lose out the *Treadle Pin* we cannot weave a shoot, neither can we add to our spiritual garment without *Humility.*

23rd.   *Temples*   *Discretion*
The *Temples* keep our cloth even so should *Discretion* guide us in all our deportment.

24th.   *Bobbin*   *Energy*
We should take hold of *Energy* to do our work as we take hold of the *Bobbin* to weave.

25th.   *Breast Beam*   *Fortitude*
We must have *Fortitude* to keep our Faith & works firm & in their station as does the *Breast Beam.*

26th.   *Upper Cloth Beam*   *Union*
The cloth passed over this *Beam* in *Union* with the lower Beam.

27th. *Mending Yarn* *Repentance*
If we break 'ie) disobey Faith it must be mended with *Repentance* as the Warp is mended with the *Mending Yarn.*

28th. *Pins* to mend with *Simplicity*
Simplicity seems small yet exceeding necessary as are those *Pins.*

29th. *Knife* *Testimony of Truth*
The *Knife* cuts off all Frags & Threads that disfigure our garment as does a sharp *Testimony.*

30th. *Spindle* *Love*
Love to the gospel & to our own souls (as well as to others) must move our Faith & Conscience into action as the Shuttle goes with the aid of the *Spindle.*

31st. *Oil* *Peace.*
Peace maketh all smooth as does *Oil.*

32nd. *Quill Box* *Innocence*
Innocence must be attached to virtue to assist in keeping our conscience safe as the *Quill Box* is attached to the Loom to put our Quills in.

33rd. *Back Rod* *Redemption*
When we have found *Redemption* our garment is woven & the *Back Rod* is at the end of the piece.

34th. *Yarn Beam* *Salvation*
The *Yarn Beam* is the largest thing on the Loom which must be *Salvation.*

Manuscripts may turn up in the most unlikely places. When one of the workmen at Hancock Village was repairing a high swivel shop stool, he had to remove the worn leather from the seat. In the wood shavings which served as a cushion he found a sheet of paper on which was written a "Poem." It was barely decipherable but it revealed, in its pathetic lines, the secret unhappiness of one man who never should have been a Shaker. On one side was the legend, "To the Finder. Remember me." Charles B. (Brown). The poem was dated June 30, 1871:

> When this is found most likely
> I within my grave shall sleep
> And ore my head light zephyrs lull
> To [make] the mourner weep.
> But may it be in some far clime
> Remote from these Bare hills
> In some lo[w] del or shining nook
> Or by the running Rills.
> For these Bare hills I have a dred
> My soul disdaineth myrth
> And O may god deliver me
> From living a Hell on earth.

XIX

COLLECTING, WRITING AND FRIENDSHIPS

In his introduction to W.H. Hudson's *Birds and Man,* Edward Garnett refers to the naturalist's human perspective: ". . . he does not isolate his subject, which always produces a dry and meagre effect, but shows it naturally through the medium of human interests and associations."

In much the same way the pieces in our collection—our subject, our "birds"—cannot be isolated, as they might have been had we bought them from shops or dealers. There are few items which are not associated with a person, or with some adventure among these gentle folk. We found them among the people who had made them and in the rooms where they had been used so long.

Nor was there a question of bargaining over price. The transaction would be prefaced by talk with some good sister or brother, talk about many things in the Shaker world, the Shaker past. We would then depart with our purchase, to which, for good measure, "trivia" had often been added: tools, a bonnet, a kerchief, a basket, a mirror frame, perhaps some stereographs, and often fruit, vegetables or flowers. It was more an exchange of greetings than a business deal.

Our unique sideboard, for example, calls to mind a trip we took to Canterbury, the bountiful luncheon prepared for us by the kitchen sisters, the loading of the piece on the top of our car, and the drive homeward in the cool fresh air under the stars. One of the few brethren left at New Lebanon guided us to the loft of an old stone shop to show us and sell us a shoemaker's bench, with little dovetailed tin-bottomed drawers and all its equipment including the Shaker asthma powder on which some cobbler once depended for relief. In the same way we cannot think of our large maple loom without seeing Sister Sadie Neale, alone in the great wash-house of the Church family at New Lebanon, weaving a multicolored rug in the pale morning light. One of our most prized pieces, a low splay-legged table, will always mean

Eldress Prudence Stickney; it was standing in a dark passage in a basement buttery or bake-room, and with it came her blessing. Sister Sarah Collins is inseparable from many of our chairs, the records of the chair industry, and a three-drawer cupboard-counter. In our mind's eye, as we contemplate a delicate candlestand which Homer Keyes once called "a perfect symbol" of Shaker craftsmanship, is Sister Lillian Barlow of the Second family, where it was made. The carefully constructed model on which the patent was secured for the Shaker "wash mill" evokes the figure of Sister Marguerite Frost and the quiet school room at Canterbury where we found it. In whatever room it is placed, our curly maple tailoress counter still stands—in our memory —in the sunlit shop of the South family at Watervliet, whither we were guided, in the last years of that community, by Sister Jennie Wells. And when Eldress Anna Case, in that same family, gave us one of her choicest possessions, a piece of Mother Ann's dress, she gave us her confidence, her affection, an unfading memory.

Many of our finest pieces came from Hancock; and as we live with them, dust and polish and arrange them, we are carried back to the spacious, immaculately clean rooms of the Church family dwelling and the graciousness of Sister Alice, through whom the acquisitions came. Recalling, in contrast, such experiences as the one when we obtained our X-trestle ironing table only after much haggling with a contentious caretaker at Enfield, Connecticut, we realize how fortunate we were to deal with the Shakers themselves.

How can one *fully* appreciate the beauty and significance of an old piece of furniture unless one knows something about the persons it served? In another place we have tried to suggest how helpful many of them were: Sadie, Alice, Rosetta, Sarah and the rest. There were others who contributed, in varying measure, to our knowledge and understanding: Eldress Josephine Wilson, Elder Arthur Bruce and Sisters Marguerite Frost and Edith Green at Canterbury; Anna Case and Jennie Wells at Watervliet; Elder Walter Shepherd of the New Lebanon North family; and Eldress Fannie Estabrook at Hancock. We were often impetuous, and doubtless, in our eagerness to learn and to find, we must have interfered with the daily routine. But we invariably found our Shaker friends hospitable and patient.

They were the rule. Admittedly, there were exceptions—members of the order, sometimes in positions of authority, who misunderstood our motives. Jealousies existed within the society as well as without giving rise to rumors that we were exploiting an innocent people.

The basic attitude, however, was one of trust. How reassured we were, after our first major publication—*The Community Industries of the Shakers* (1932)—to receive the following letter from Eldress Prudence Stickney of Sabbathday Lake:

The shoemaker's shop at the Second family of the Church Order, New Lebanon. The cobbler's bench and floor stand for candles were from a brethren's shop at the Second family. The smaller candlestand was made at the Church family. The early lasts were also Shaker-made.

Eldress Anna Case

The low maple splay-legged table at left was used in the washhouse at Sabbathday Lake, Maine.

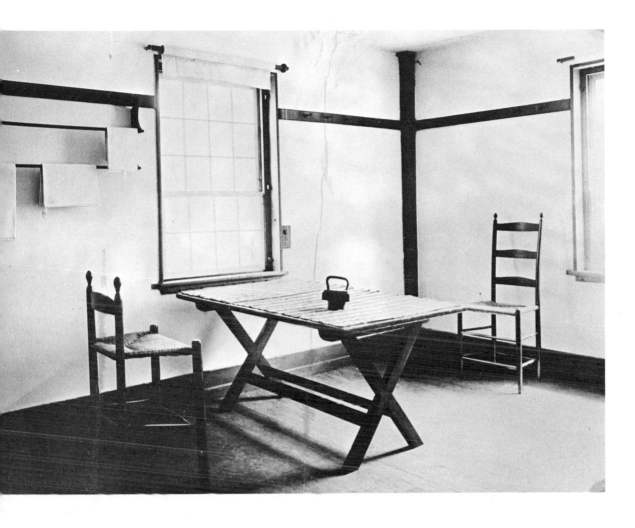

X-trestle ironing table used at the Enfield (Connecticut) community.

Ministry sideboard, Canterbury, N.H.

Everyone says how beautifully and sweet they have mentioned the old days that the world cannot understand, and so we all say it is wonderful. . . . You have been so interested and so careful in selecting everything that the world should know more of our religious life, and preserving the sacred things. All credit is due you for your noble work.

After her visit to our home in Pittsfield we were doubly reassured by the following note:

One of my happiest memories is of you two dear ones. How I did enjoy the time spent with you. To know and feel the deep reverence you have for the old Shaker things, did my heart good. Every touch was full of love and devotion for those who have given their lives in full consecration to God's work. . . .

Though some Shakers realized the importance of preserving their heritage, it is doubtful how far our efforts would have carried without recognition from the world outside— really outside, for locally it seemed that the Believers were still considered a peculiar people with no important bearing on our national life and thought.

The first person of influence to sense the values inherent in Shaker culture and craftsmanship, and to encourage our undertaking, was Homer Keyes, whose counsel we have elsewhere acknowledged. Through William Winter, an amateur photographer from Schenectady, N.Y., whom we met one day taking pictures at Mount Lebanon, the State Museum in Albany became interested in assembling a collection, and subsequently commissioned us to write a pamphlet, and later a monograph, on the economic principles and industrial products of the order. This was a step forward, since it gave us an objective to study and collate the vast amount of material –journals, daybooks and other records—we had already collected.

The writing of *The Community Industries of the Shakers* was a useful discipline; it taught us to adhere to evidence, to primary sources, and not to present as truth what was merely hearsay. The monograph leaned heavily on records, which sometimes were at variance with tradition. It was an accepted fact, for instance, that chair making was an early industry, but no one, not even the Shakers, had any idea when it started. Some would say, vaguely, "before the Civil War," or "perhaps early in the last century." In this case it was exciting to find, in a worn old ledger, entries of chair sales as early as 1789. Again, we had been told that the Shakers, having separated from the world, were entirely self-sufficient; and not till we had examined their records did we discover that they were a very practical folk, that they often bartered goods and frequently bought from the world if cheaper or more convenient. We learned that their furniture, though distinct, was not without its antecedents, just as we learned that their songs sometimes had secular origins, or origins in other religions. Only their medicinal extracts were prepared *in vacuo*.

The same was true of many inventions with which they were credited. Some were, indeed, original devices, the result of the special needs of a communal economy. Others were "improvements," born of the desire to excel the world. Still others, we found, were outright patentees. A few examples will illustrate the pitfalls into which the unwary scholar could fall. The story had been repeated so often that Sarah Babbitt of the Harvard community was the inventor of cut nails and the circular saw that it was generally accepted as true. Isaac Youngs was supposed to have invented metal pens about 1819. The Shakers were also credited with inventing planing and washing machines as well as the electro-therapeutic device used in their nurse-shops for shocking patients. And so on. Research revealed, however, that cut nails for shingling and lathing antedated the Shaker industry; that metal pens were probably invented by a Baltimore jeweler about 1800; that the "Shaker" revolving timber-planes were originally patented by a non-Shaker named David Smith; and that the "wash mill" patented by David Parker of Canterbury in 1858 was based on a model which Sylvester Noble of Hoosick, N.Y. had patented as early as 1810. Noble sold the right to make and use his wash mill to the Shakers for a nominal sum.

It was the electrostatic machine, however, which "shocked" us first. We had been assured that it was an ingenious concept springing, fully developed, from some Shaker intellect. Hesitant about accepting the attribution, we wrote to an authority on electro-therapy, Dr. William Bierman of the New York Physical Therapy Society. He replied courteously and at length to the effect that the use of electricity in medicine had been demonstrated back in the eighteenth century by John Wesley, Benjamin Franklin and others, and that early in the nineteenth century Galvani, an Italian physicist, had shown that electric currents (Galvanic currents) had a stimulating effect on the nerves of the body. It was improbable, therefore, that the Shakers had actually invented the machine, though it is noteworthy that they constructed and used them as early as the first decade of the 19th century. Dr. Bierman's letter was a timely warning against hasty conclusions.

The publication of the book on industries was followed by several exhibitions, a small one in Boston that attracted little attention, another at the Albany State Museum which was more successful, and a third at the Berkshire Museum in Pittsfield, which was destined to have far-reaching consequences. For it was here, through the instrumentality of its imaginative director, Miss Laura Bragg, that we became acquainted with Mrs. Juliana Force, the director of the Whitney Museum in New York City.

Mrs. Force had a collection of Shaker furniture which she had obtained from a dealer in Ridgefield, Connecticut, who had bought certain pieces from us at a time when we were under obligation to sell. The dealer, naturally, had not revealed the source of his purchases, so it was with great surprise, at the dinner which Miss Bragg gave for us before the opening of the exhibit, that Mrs. Force learned that we were the original owners. Deeply interested as she was in promoting American art and craftsmanship, she was avid to know all about the Shakers and their work. She came to our home; we visited the Hancock and New Lebanon communities; we talked from early morning till late at night. Once convinced of the value of our work she assumed personal sponsorship, granting us a subsidy which continued for two years.

Though the grant came to an end, her support continued, for in November, 1935, the Whitney Museum sponsored an exhibition of our collection in New York, where it received wide and favorable comment.

"Please understand," she wrote in February, 1935 "how badly I feel about your work being interrupted by the withdrawal of the little sum which you have used to such advantage in furthering the work we have so believed in. . . ."

Much of the subsidy was used in preparing a book-length study: *Shaker Furniture, The Craftsmanship of an American Communal Sect.* Mrs. Force also aided Winter, our photographer, and for three years we were all actively engaged on this project.

Our choice for publisher was the Yale University Press. I had done my graduate work and received my doctorate at Yale, and the press had seriously considered publishing my thesis. We had met Carl Purington Rollins, printer to the university, whose appreciation for fine craftsmanship in the William Morris tradition extended to the furniture of the Shakers. This made the Yale Press a logical choice. We were confident that under Carl's personal supervision it would be a beautiful book. Many were the conferences, at the Whitney, at Homer's apartment, at Yale. And when the book finally appeared, in 1937, with congratulations from Carl that "our baby had at last been born," it even surpassed our expectations. It later received an award as one of the "Fifty Best Books of the Year."

The Whitney show opened up another activity—participation in a federal art project which is discussed in the following chapter. More fruitful, however, was the encouragement that both Homer and Juliana gave us to study another aspect of the Shaker culture, namely the songs, dances and rituals of the sect. It was Mrs. Force who recommended me for a Guggenheim Fellowship for 1937-38, with

"The Religious Arts of the Shakers" as its project. We had previously published one article, in *The Magazine Antiques,* on the so-called "inspirational" drawings and paintings of the Believers, a number of which had been exhibited, for the first time, in the Whitney show. Appreciation followed. Dr. Ruth Benedict, Department of Anthropology at Columbia University, referred to the inspirationals as "a careful and important collection of the most distinctive and delightful folk art that it has been my privilege to see from America."

In our library there was also a wealth of material, never before explored, on the "gifts" and rites which characterized Shaker worship, including the mysterious "love feasts" on the holy mounts. We had collected many manuscript hymnals and song books dating from the 1820's which we had shown to Dr. Martha W. Beckwith, head of the American Folklore Foundation. On November 23, 1936, she sent us her appraisal:

> Your special field seems an unbelievably rich one. I have sometimes wondered whether the Shaker ritual did not contain some genuine folk material, but could not have predicted anything so interesting as your collection . . .
>
> When I first undertook this field of Folklore (American native song) some skeptical European scholars said, "But you have no folklore in America." Since then I have been overwhelmed by the discovery of so much material buried under in the haste for Americanization and modernization, here in America.

Encouraged by such authorities, and later by Professors George Herzog of Columbia and George Pullen Jackson of Vanderbilt, we plunged into this new and untried field, using appropriate material from the copious notes we had shown to Dr. Benedict. The immediate incentive, of course, was the Guggenheim grant.

The study of early Shaker religious songs was, and continues to be an exciting venture. Notation was in letters—not in code, as Clara Endicott Sears once surmised—but for a person not trained in musicology, it was difficult at first to transcribe the literal into standard round-note form. Isaac Youngs' *A Short Abridgement of the Rules of Music* helped, but there was still need for collaboration.

This came from an unexpected quarter. Professor Jackson had read an article which we had published in *The Musical Quarterly,* writing us of his interest in a school of "white spirituals," chiefly of southern provenance. Questioning certain statements in the above article, he offered constructive suggestions for revision. Correspondence was followed by a visit to our farm in Richmond, where we brought out all our song books and related materials. For several days it was, on our part, a learning period of great value.

How clearly we recall the walks along the country roads, with

George Pullen chewing tobacco, spinning yarns and expatiating on his experiences collecting revival songs and others in the South, and later, the scene at Fraunces' Tavern in New York, where he conducted "The Old Harp Singers" of Nashville, a memorable concert followed by informal singing in the bar. His frequent letters were informative and delightful, the product of an independent mind which had not lost touch with the folk spirit. Sometimes they would contain a humorous anecdote, again a serious query, and occasionally a folk song of his own composition. With scholarship he combined the warm generosity of a friend.

Two other musician-scholars collaborated in arranging the tunes for *The Gift to be Simple,* the title we gave to the finished work. One was Tom Ryan, whom we had met through the Armin Landecks, and with whom we worked one summer in Richmond. The other was Conrad Held, a friend of long standing whom we had first known as a member of the South Mountain Quartet in Pittsfield. Most of the arrangements in the book, and all of them in a contribution we made to Schirmer's Folk Song Series, were the work of this dynamic, enthusiastic musician who truly had "the gift of song."

The Gift To Be Simple was strictly a labor of love. But in terms of personal satisfaction, and as a stepping stone to further adventures, it had great rewards. One of the songs became the recurrent theme in Aaron Copland's *Appalachian Spring,* which we first heard, with pride in having had some part in its creation, when it was played by the Boston Symphony Orchestra at Tanglewood, and again when it was danced in New York by Martha Graham's company. "Simple Gifts" and other songs were first recorded on tape by a choral group at Scarborough School, where I was then teaching. The fine recording made on the occasion of a "Shaker Festival" at Smith College in 1960, in which students from Amherst and Smith participated, was subsequently used as an epilogue to lectures at Williamsburg and Dearborn.

Latent in our minds, for years, was the desire to do a definitive history of the Shaker movement. The studies of industry, furniture and songs were specialized monographs. We had amassed reams of notes bearing on Shaker history. True, our collection of artifacts *was* history in the broad sense of the word. But as the years went by and the collection found no permanent repository, it seemed mandatory to organize, between covers, what knowledge we possessed. Whatever happened to the collection we would feel better if our labors could be thus consummated. The book would be, as Conrad had a character say in *Lord Jim,* "something of me, the best."

It is difficult to determine just when an idea is first translated into action. Experiences of all kinds accumulate to a point when one says, now we must stop talking and start doing. People like Homer and

Juliana played initial roles, as did Henry Allen Moe, of the Guggenheim Foundation; Jackson and Ruth Benedict; Francis Taylor, who gave us an exhibition in 1938-39; Ananda Coomaraswamy, of the Boston Museum of Fine Arts, who attended our Pittsfield show, wrote a perceptive review of our furniture book, and sent a pamphlet on the exhibition to his friend Gandhi; Mark Van Doren, who wrote a wonderful review in *The Nation* called "Religion in Wood"; Charles MacLean Andrews of Yale and Rufus Jones of Haverford; and Bernard De Voto, editor of *The Saturday Review of Literature,* who wrote that he could "imagine no more interesting or more valuable project" than a history of the Shakers.

Inspiration came from other sources, from such appreciators of what was fine and beautiful in the American tradition as Cornelia Parker, Edna Greenwood, Catherine White, Arthur Wallace Peach in Vermont, and our early friend Frank Lawton of Shirley Center, Massachusetts, at whose home, during the years of World War I, I first saw samples of Shaker craftsmanship. One of the first letters of appreciation came from him, early in 1934 with the comment, "Your Shaker book *(The Community Industries)* is a classic, and very precious to us . . . Let our thanks be a Song without Words. . . ."

With such encouragement playing upon our inner urge, a point was reached, in the latter part of the depression decade, when work was started. Four or five chapters were completed, which won tentative approval from an editor at the Oxford University Press. Then the project was laid aside. Other matters interfered. After *The Gift To Be Simple* was published the war came. There was also the education of the children and a new teaching position demanding full time for nine months of the year. We had bought a ten-acre farm with our first royalty check from Yale, and the dilapidated, eighteenth century farmhouse badly needed repairs. The manuscript lay untouched. There seemed to be no time to write and at times no incentive.

Then interest revived. One summer, late in the forties, we decided, almost on the spur of the moment, to put the history through. There were evidences everywhere of an awakening interest in Americana: folk art and music, religion, minority movements. Constance Rourke had published a germinal work on *The Roots of American Culture,* and Marguerite Melcher had brought out her book on *The Shaker Adventure. Life* and *The New Yorker* had run articles on the sect. The furniture book had gone into a third edition. The New York Historical Association had invited us to organize an exhibit at Cooperstown which attracted widespread attention.

For three summers we concentrated on the history—to the detriment of the kitchen garden at Richmond and other pleasurable matters. At the end of school vacation in 1950 it was finished, and on a never-to-be-forgotten day the following winter we heard that Oxford would accept it. It had been read by Carleton Hayes and others at Cooperstown. The Oxford reader liked it. It had met all the tests! That morning at Scarborough School, when Carroll Bowen, an Oxford editor, phoned to report that the Press would be happy to publish it, I am sure that my behavior was such that faculty and students alike thought I had taken leave of my senses.

As in the case of Yale, collaboration with Leona Capeless, an editor, and John Begg, art editor, was an experience in fulfillment.

After each of our books was published, letters arrived revealing how many people had had some contact with or some story to tell about "The Believers in Christ's Second Appearing."

Some of the correspondence has been with people we never met. Such was the case with J.P. MacLean, the grand old man of Shaker research in the West, author of *The Shakers of Ohio* and *A Bibliography of Shaker Literature,* an inscribed copy of which he sent us with a note written in an unsteady hand; Mrs. John Spring, an early collector; Dr. Walter Prince of the Society of Psychic Research, who became interested years ago in Shaker spiritualism; Lee Emerson Deets, whose interest was the Hutterites; and Henri Desroche, who was writing in France a history of *Les Shakers Americains.*

Informal sketches of Shakers by Peter Neagoe made, in the early 1930's, on the margins of his drawings for a Shaker catalogue entitled Products of Intelligence and Diligence.

Correspondence also led to personal acquaintance. Once we traced the drawings in a Shaker catalogue to Peter Neagoe, author of *Storm, Easter Sun,* etc., an immigrant who had spent part of his boyhood at the North family in New Lebanon and with whom we had a most pleasant visit in New York. A prolonged correspondence preceded the visit of Daryl Chase who was writing his thesis on the Shakers.

In a related catagory are a few people we came to know as sharers of our interest: Alice Winchester, who became editor of *Antiques* following the death of Homer Keyes; Ezra Stoller, who took pictures of our Shaker farm for *The Ladies Home Journal;* Mary Margaret McBride, with whom we were associated in a radio broadcast; Doris Humphrey, whom we met after a performance of her *Dance of the Chosen;* John Peter of *Look* magazine; the late Caroline Piercy, whose interest in the Shakers led to the founding of a museum at Shaker Heights, Ohio, and the writing of two books on the subject. These and many more formed a network of common understanding as we went forward with our many Shaker studies.

XX

THE AMERICAN INDEX OF DESIGN

The exhibit at the Whitney Museum of American Art was held at the height, or rather depth, of the depression era. One of its by-products, aside from the interest it awakened in Shaker art and craftsmanship, was the compilation of a permanent record of Shaker design, on the part of the federal government, as a relief project. The American Index of Design was organized as one phase of the Works Progress Administration, its immediate purpose being to utilize the skills of unemployed artists and photographers in many parts of the country. Shaker craftsmanship was a new discovery, and it seemed to the authorities so excellent in quality and so comprehensive in scope that they decided to make its documentation a major section of the Index. The work, and its progress, were to be (we were told) under our own responsible control.

The idea was a good one. Devoted to the idea of perpetuating, through various media, the forms and colors of Shaker furniture, architecture and household objects, we entered into the project with enthusiasm. At our home in Pittsfield, where most of our collection was then housed, we welcomed the painters, costume designers and photographers who had been assigned to the theme. They were serious, deserving people, grateful for the opportunity to work, and we became accustomed to their using our home as a studio. We put them to work drawing and painting pictures of chairs, tables, chests, beds, oval boxes and other small joinery, shop furnishings, braids, fabrics, costumes, iron and tinware, baskets—all kinds of handicraft. They were not equally competent, of course. Some had difficulty in making a box look oval. Only one artist could draw a chair well, catch its refinement of line. They had difficulty with color and proportion. There were times, indeed, when we thought it would be easier to cut down the height of a table or stand than to struggle with an artist so that the dimensions looked right. They all labored diligently, however, and after the day's work was done we had good times together.

What we hadn't counted on, however, were the supervisors assigned by absentee overlords to check on what we were doing. These administrators knew little or nothing about the material, or about the special conditions under which we had obtained the cooperation of the Shakers. Their function was to select the artists, outline the program, document the completed work, select what was to be exhibited, and then exhibit it—in Boston, New York and other metropolitan centers.

That was where the trouble began. Though we alone were well acquainted with the field, we lacked full authority. Things constantly went wrong. We had guided the artists to various communities, introducing them to our Shaker friends and arranging—often a delicate task—to have them work in the family dwellings and shops. At that time there were societies in four states. Hancock was in Massachusetts, our home state, and just across the New York state line were two other extant colonies: New Lebanon, the largest community in the East, and Watervliet, the original home of the sect. But when the authorities decided that the project should be conducted by states we found it difficult, and then *verboten,* to work in any state but our own. This meant that we would be confined to the Hancock settlement and have no control over what was done in the other two.

That was irritating but not disastrous since our collection had originally come from all over New England and New York state. We soon discovered, however, that drawings and paintings which did not do justice to a given object were being retained over our objections and exhibited as true indices of a culture which always sought perfection.

This was not all. Material loaned to accompany the exhibits was misplaced or returned in poor shape. And when we visited the exhibitions and read the documentation—which had also begun to appear in pamphlets and periodicals—we were appalled by the errors. Through ignorance, indifference or carelessness in processing the illustrations which accumulated in the Federal Art offices, our work was going out into the world under false colors. Protests availed little. The errors stood and presumably still remain in government files.

The end of our part in the project was inevitable. In our attempt to achieve high standards of artistry and accuracy we were defeated. Supervisors resented our criticism, especially when, after initial failures to get results, it was directed to higher authorities. The "brass" stuck together. We were called "uncooperative." And finally, when the situation became intolerable, we received a telegram one morning, from the director in Washington, notifying us that we had been fired—"terminated" the word was, "without prejudice." The discharge was illegally made retroactive, with salary due us withheld. A little later we were threatened by a visit from the "bureau of criminal investigation" if we

```
                                    HOLGER CAHILL, DIRECTOR
                                    FEDERAL ART PROJECT

                                         W.&P. PROJECTS

                                    WP 5-5

DAY LETTER                          OCTOBER 5, 1936


EDWARD ANDREWS
42 CLINTON AVENUE
PITTSFIELD, MASSACHUSETTS

THIS WILL NOTIFY YOU THAT YOUR SERVICES WERE TERMINATED WITHOUT PREJUDICE

AS OF SEPTEMBER FOURTEEN NINETEEN HUNDRED THIRTY SIX  stop  YOU WILL BE PAID

UP TO AND INCLUDING OCTOBER SECOND NINETEEN HUNDRED THIRTY SIX DATE OF

ENDING OF ACCRUED ANNUAL LEAVE  stop  YOU WILL BE CONTINUED ON WITHOUT PAY

BASIS TO OCTOBER THIRTY ONE NINETEEN HUNDRED THIRTY SIX -




                                    HOLGER CAHILL, DIRECTOR
                                    FEDERAL ART PROJECT
Parker/ g
```

did not return a duplicate set of photographs which had been presented to us as a gift from one of the directors of the project.

The fault was in a bureaucracy jealously guarding its prerogatives and indifferent to advice. Much good work was accomplished—the Index is a valuable source of material on Shaker design. But never having been properly edited—even after our final appeal before an illustrated book went to press—pitfalls remain for the artist and historian in the future.

XXI

HOMER EATON KEYES

Homer Eaton Keyes spent the Labor Day weekend of 1938 at our saltbox farmhouse in Richmond, Massachusetts. On Saturday afternoon he was guided to the back road—No. 10 in the old maps, now Dublin Road—which was used only by an occasional farmer, or a commuter who knew it as a shortcut to and from the city. He stayed till Tuesday, anxious to avoid the holiday traffic and postpone his return to the tensions of New York. Except for one excursion to a neighboring quarry pond and a brief siesta on the sunny terrace, he was content to rest in an easy chair before the Shaker stove, to smoke and talk.

Conversation turned to many topics—seldom to the problems that convulsed the world, often to the themes he loved, the projects he had planned for fall and winter: articles, lectures, the long-postponed work on Lowestoft. His body was tired, his wisdom mellow, but his spirit was as young as ever. Mornings, afternoons, well into the evening we talked, now about Lowestoft and Staffordshire, now about pewter and iron-ware, now of furniture, but chiefly of American folk art and the recurrent subject of the nature of art itself. All craftsmanship he would call art. Art, he would insist, was like sweat—it comes when one strives, constructs, works hard and inevitably toward a goal. The aim might be a humble one: a good stone wall, a garden that would yield its full bounty, a rug well braided. To paint a landscape, a still life, a portrait, was art too if completely done, but not more so than taking good care of trees, say, or expending pains on some simple utilitarian object like a box or kitchen utensil. Art, for him, permeated every aspect of life; it was life that made art real.

He took a lively interest, as all his friends knew, in the art of cookery. Before meals he presided over the wood stove in the kitchen, concocting delicious meals from simple ingredients. Vinegar in the swirling water kept compact the whites of the eggs we poached for breakfast. We christened a new blend of coffee. The herbs used with the pot roast made of dinner a royal feast. We learned the secret of polenta, new ways of preparing vegetables from our garden. The meals were New England, but different because of his presence.

Sunday morning, after breakfast, he busied himself sketching glimpses of those rooms which caught his fancy: corners, vistas, studies in angles. The little chamber in which he slept, the one we called the "Kitchen sister's room," particularly pleased him. Quiet and peaceful, furnished only with a cot, a small chest, a bench and a trestle table with books, it was to him a "St. Jerome's study—a chamber of innocent dreams." In the living room he liked the low wood-burning stove, with its narrow angled pipe; the simple three-slat chairs around the hutch table; the long Shaker settee; the monastic effect of the sturdy beams and white, rough-plastered walls; the green-blue chair rail, doors and window casings; and in the evening the triangular shadow cast by the light of candles in the Shaker sconces. The sketches were to serve as guides for photographic studies—they caught his feeling for the place, revealing his mood as well as his artistry.

Shaker Farm was "a sanctuary." Here, in the country quiet, "where people could be themselves," he was at peace with himself. When the visit was over, and he drove off down the country road that Tuesday morning, we had the premonition that we would not see again a benefactor who had become one of our closest friends.

The "Kitchen sister's room"

157

XXII

MISCELLANEA

A PROFESSOR'S CHAIRS

June 1952

At Amherst College, back in 1912, I took a course in zoology under Professor John Tyler, whom the students used to call "Tip" ("Tippecanoe and Tyler too.") There were many stories about him, like this one:

"Why is Tip like the Central Vermont Railroad?"

"Because his ties are all worn out."

He was a brilliant scientist, highly respected in his field, but he rather enjoyed his reputation of being something of a character. One day in class—we were studying biological mutations at the time—he remarked, as he stroked his long bald scalp with a pencil, that he himself was a rare specimen, one of the few humans with dolichocephalic skulls who was not insane. He planned to will his brain to a scientific institution.

How he became interested in the Shakers we never knew. Perhaps he regarded them, too, as rare biological specimens. The notes taken in that course have long since been lost, but his gleanings in another field we found forty years after I sat at his feet in that old lecture hall. It seems that early in the century he had made several trips to New Lebanon, selecting with the discrimination of a true scientist "specimens" of Shaker craftsmanship, chiefly chairs and lap desks. At his death they had passed into the possession of the Jones Library, a private institution in Amherst in which he had a particular interest. We had a small exhibit there once, and the Tyler pieces were brought out of storage to supplement our contribution.

Delicate Shaker chairs, especially rockers, are not the ideal furnishing of a library, so in due course the professor's collection was offered to us. On a sunny Monday in June we drove to the old college town and loaded eight of the best chairs and two exquisite lap desks into our car, particularly happy in the acquisitions since they were associated with a great scholar and beloved teacher.

158

"Tip's" interest in the Shakers bore fruit in another form. His daughter, Alice, became steeped in the subject of dissenting American sects, and later, as a professor at the University of Minnesota, published a scholarly work entitled "Freedom's Ferment."

On the way home from Amherst that day we tried to extend our luck by looking up a country dealer-collector who had purchased from us, years before, a Shaker trestle table. It was one of two we had found in the basement of a house formerly occupied by a Shaker family. We had paid little for the two pieces, and had sold this one at a profit, a transaction which finally convinced my mother that in buying Shaker antiques we were not foolish spendthrifts. Now we hoped we could re-purchase it, as we did the other table which we had also unwisely sold. It was now in a sort of cabin deep in the woods back of the dealer's house, and we reasoned that since the owner was probably not well off—he worked as a common laborer on the town roads—we might persuade him to part with it.

But he was not at home. An old woman peered out of the window of his roadside cottage, but otherwise the place was deserted. We were skeptical about reaching him by mail, for the mail box, a battered tin box stuck awry on a pole, seemed never to have been used. For all we knew the person we sought, an eccentric who was also a connoisseur, may have been back in the cabin, sitting alone and reading at the table we coveted. He loved books, too.

THE CALL OF THE GARDEN

July 1954

Was it Emerson or Thoreau who observed how hard it was to stay indoors and write on a summer day when the carrots needed weeding? Was it some primeval urge or escape from discipline that caused the conflict? Today, as often before in our sixteen summers at Shaker Farm, the situation arose. The alternatives were working on the libretto of an opera or thinning the neglected rows of carrots and beets. The scare-crow, too, should be taken down, now that the corn was well advanced. Spinach should be cut, and if we were to have an herb bed back of the cowshed it was high time to spade the ground and line off the paths. The wood-box also was empty.

Weren't these chores more important than the libretto—the fate of Sister Eunice, torn between the call of the Shaker heaven and the desire to join her Aaron in the world? When the carrots were thinned, the results could be seen. A sense of deep satisfaction would accompany the creation of an herb garden. Eunice's problem was unreal. Whichever path we had her take, it would be a decision regarding an imaginary being. We must justify that decision, which required mental effort—on a summer's day. What difference, after all, did it make what Eunice did? You may say there was a challenge in bringing to life a lovely Shaker sister. If we made her live, and resolved her dilemma, how much greater the reward than modifying, ever so slightly, the environment of a farmstead.

There was only one answer. God was in our garden this morning. The Kentucky Wonders were putting forth their feelers; the bean poles were a foot away, but an Unseen Force was guiding the groping tendrils in the right direction. To tend the garden, to assist in the miracle of growth, seemed a greater creative act.

CANTERBURY REVISITED

July 1954

Sixteen years had elapsed since we last visited the Canterbury Shakers. When we drove up there, on a hot July day in 1954, we found that this lovely hilltop community, whose membership was about three hundred at the time of the Civil War, now was reduced to fifteen, all sisters. We met five of them: Marguerite Frost, whom we had known best (we'd sent her a Christmas greeting every year); Rebecca Hathaway, whose domain was the cannery—a Flemish-like room where, on our last visit, tomatoes in green and red bowls and vegetable trays were being prepared for the steaming kettles; Ada, who was to guide us on a tour of the buildings; Edith Clark, who tended the store, where "fancy goods," now limited to the handiwork of a few sisters, were still being sold; and Helena, the last surviving member of a famed Shaker quartet, who, despite her advanced age, was still busy in her shop with needlework and the painting of pictures of the Canterbury scene. Sister Marguerite, who presided over the "nurse shop," was our hostess.

It was a moving experience to find oneself again among the Shakers: to see them still pursuing what was left of the traditional occupations; to find them still wearing their net caps and bonnets; and to hear them speaking of Mother Ann and the first witnesses as though these saints were present with them. Marguerite was fond of collecting stones and had brought one from the site at Harvard, Massachusetts, where Father James Whittaker had been so cruelly abused.

"Sixteen years is too long a time for people with the same interest to stay away from each other," she said. "Barriers can be set up. It is important, when there are differences of opinion, to talk things out." The remark, we surmised, was in reference to our latest book, *The People Called Shakers,* certain passages of which some of the Shakers had misinterpreted. On her bookshelf were our other books; she felt we had done justice to the industrial life of the Shakers, their furniture, even their songs and strange rituals. We sensed that she was reserved, however, and unhappy about our history which she did not possess but had "scanned."

Faith tried to reassure Marguerite, pointing out that a historian must be honestly objective and in the case at issue must present clearly the basis on which the Shakers were once misunderstood and persecuted. What certain Shakers objected to was the use of quotations from Mary Dyer's book, *A Portraiture of Shakerism,* in which the Believers were charged, in court and out, with various offenses. The protracted litigation was a notorious one at the time, with charges and rebuttals often cancelling each other out. However, in order to show how the society was villified it was necessary to clarify the form that persecution took, to *illustrate* the charges in all their graphic detail. It wouldn't do merely to state that the Shakers were accused of mistreating children, the aged, the disobedient, etc., and let it go at that. To demonstrate how slander and malicious gossip affected the fortunes of the society, and why Mary Dyer's books found so many readers, the historian must present selections from her own statements. Otherwise the issue would have lacked documentation.

"What the Shakers believed," Faith continued, "Ted has presented in their own words, from their own writings. No one is better equipped to tell the story so justly, so completely. You may rest assured that his mind is free of any prejudice or guile. No one is more humble." After the conversation we felt that Marguerite had a better understanding of the ethics of scholarship. On our part, we welcomed the experience, and were thankful that there still existed, in the society, members with whom we could talk frankly.

On our tour with Sister Ada we visited the kitchen, bake room, herb shop, laundry and school, all deserted now except for the kitchen, where modern conveniences had supplanted the early methods of cooking, refrigeration and laundering. From Rebecca we purchased a flat-iron holder mounted on wood, which she carefully cleaned before she sold it. There was a bench in her shop which we liked, but this she would not sell; it had been made for her long ago, she said, by a brother whose craftsmanship she admired. "I am being very un-Shaker, very selfish," she admitted, "but I can not part with it now." Our call had found Rebecca busy sorting and drying catnip for the cloth "mice" sold in the shop. Tarragon still grew by her doorway, and she still prepared tarragon vinegar for domestic use. Hospitable, jovial and active for her age, this friendly soul nevertheless saddened us, for the shop and its keeper symbolized the destiny of one of the oldest Shaker industries.

There was not much to buy in the school room, where miscellaneous merchandise, mostly non-Shaker, was neatly arranged. More interesting were the herbs and plants growing wild around the "nurse shop." With a Shaker-made spade we dug up, at Marguerite's invitation, the roots of a trumpet vine and a few herbs; lemon balm, tansy, Jerusalem oak and princess pine—straggling survivors of the medicinal herb industry. The trumpet vine we have planted in back of our farmhouse.

Our talk with Marguerite, whose memory goes back to the time when she was brought to Canterbury at the age of eleven, was most rewarding. Among her Canterbury tales we shall remember was the one about Myra, an aged sister for whom it was her duty to care. Until the very last— she died at the age of 108—this "old Believer," though she was going blind, insisted on completing daily a prescribed amount of sewing of pot holders and other small items. "It is my stint," she insisted, "it must be done." "Does she ever get out of bed?" Marguerite was often asked. To which she replied, "My problem is to get her *in* bed." Myra had her coffee at five-thirty every morning the year round. The evening meal she ate regularly with the rest of the family.

The trip to the Shaker village and back was some three hundred and fifty miles. We were tired, but so refreshed in spirit that when we arrived home we sat, relaxed and content, and in our talk relived again the day.

Because it was deserted, the experiences of revisiting another community was not so satisfactory. One summer morning, three years after the last member had left the North family at New Lebanon, we drove over Lebanon mountain to see that now abandoned property. We were in a nostalgic mood. The road leading into the village past the great stone barn was quiet and peaceful. We thought we could recapture some of the spirit that always prevailed in the Novitiate Order.

What we found were only sad memories of a life that was gone. The flower gardens, once tended so faithfully by Sisters Rosetta and Masella, were going to seed, with hardly a single bloom. The lawns were overgrown with weeds. The window panes of the brethren's brick shop were shattered, and some of the windows in the two dwellings seemed to stare vacantly into space. Unable to stand such un-Shaker neglect, Faith returned to the car. But memories not beyond recall held me to the spot. I wandered about the grounds, looking into rooms which told tales of other days. Here I had often sat, talking with Rosetta about her Shaker youth. Here Elder Walter's funeral had been held. In one room I could still see Sarah Collins, in her old age, braiding rugs. Another was the canning room, still functioning when we last were there. I looked into the visitor's room from which came our unique settee, and into the shadowy hall where we found the long pine wash bench, with two cupboards beneath, which was our last purchase from the North family. I peered into the store, which I remembered as a cool, orderly shop where the sisters put out odds and ends for sale, and where they sold their candied butternuts, maple sugar cakes and sweet flag. The laundry, the carpenters' shop, the sheds were all as they had been, but empty, oh so empty, deserted of all life save a stray cat that ran into a cellar-way at the unexpected intrusion.

Why subject oneself to such sharp regret, we asked ourselves? Every member of the family was dead. We had tried and failed to preserve the fine buildings. The "North House" had played its role, with us as with the whole New Lebanon community for which it served as the "gathering order." If it was now destined to fall into decay, so be it.

We have not returned.

THE SECOND GENERATION

When the Shaker tree was small, bearing for us its first fruits, our children were also young. They all matured together, David and Ann and the tree.

It was not long after David outgrew the playpen that he developed a collector's interest in stones, fossils, Indians, stamps, birds, butterflies and later bottles, phonograph records and old books. His earliest association with our Shaker concerns was an indirect one, during the period when we were holding an exhibit at the Albany State Museum. David was entranced by the Indian artifacts; he had a tom-tom which he liked to pound while Ann, somewhat against her inclination, did a war dance around him. The Helderberg mountains west of Albany were excellent hunting grounds, we learned, for fossil shells. So one day all of us, with Dr. Charles Adams, the director of the museum, as guide, drove up to the place noted for its deposits, right on the surface of the ground. David was of course elated, frantically filling his pockets with specimens. Only after learning that the fossils were in no sense rare finds did his enthusiasm abate.

Horse chestnuts came next, at the North family. Then the South family at New Lebanon, which yielded a variety of loot, the prize find being a collection of old gramophone records, marches by Sousa, and a disc with a laughing song which he played over and over again. Bird nests, stamps, books—all could be found somewhere on the premises or in unoccupied rooms. Shaker pamphlets were items to add to his "library," though he much preferred illustrated books or such out of the way imprints as the one with lurid lithographs, in color, of a drunkard's stomach! Gradually his taste improved, and he started collecting the bottles, jars and vials used in the Shaker medicinal herb industry. His interest in craftsmanship was yet to come.

There were intimations, however, when he was only eleven or twelve years old. We were holding our first large exhibit at the Berkshire Museum in Pittsfield, and on the afternoon of the opening had left him at home with strict instructions that he be kept within bounds. But David knew what was up, and he knew the ropes, for the museum was one of his favorite haunts. He slipped away, and in the midst of the reception showed up, unkempt but triumphant. On his arm was the president of the museum's board, a distinguished lady whom he proceeded to guide through the show, discoursing knowledgeably on its contents!

Now David has, in his home, an exhibit of his own, proud to live with those pieces—chairs, cupboards, cases of drawers, stands and benches, an ironing table, etc.—which we have given to him and his wife Phyllis. With him, as with us, an interest had its birth and then its growth into mature appreciation.

With Ann, the story had milder overtones. She was named after her grandmother, Ann Knott, who came to America from Manchester, England, and who was named, according to family tradition, after Mother Ann Lee, the Manchester prophetess.

There was nothing prophetic about Ann's first experiences with things Shaker for she seemed indifferent to what we collected. When she was in elementary school we once purchased at the West Pittsfield colony a child's red cloak, and after some opposition, persuaded her one winter's day to wear it to school. It was warm. It was becoming. But as an experiment in promoting non-conformity we should have known it wouldn't work. Ann came home at noon in tears, tore off the cloak, stamped on it, releasing her pent-up emotions in an angry outburst.

It didn't help when visitors, on occasion, patted her or David on the head with the remark, "How's the little Shaker girl today?" or "How's the little Shaker lad?" It became even more difficult when they were subjected to abstruse questioning, put on the mat as it were, with the assumption that anyone in the Andrews family should be something of an authority. The teen-age period must have been trying for them both.

But Ann also outgrew her prejudices, and eventually, after years away from home, came back to the subject with a fresh point of view. With a home of her own she now shares her brother's conviction that in its union of beauty and utility there is nothing to compare with the furnishings their parents collected when they were young.

SUMMER APPLES

August 1957

Strange how often happenings at the farm relate to the Shakers. Yesterday we went to our friends the Cranes for eggs, and saw a basket of early apples on the back stoop. Carl, a long time retainer of the Crane family, was there, and gave us permission to pick up all we wanted in the hill orchard. He called them "Red-birds," a variety no one seemed to know anything about; the nursery man who sold him the stock claimed they were superior to the Red Astrakans, tarter, more tasty. We filled a bag from the ground. The apples lay in beds of mint, and the soft air had a fragrance indescribably sweet.

Wondering what kind of apples they really were, we consulted Downing's *The Fruits and Fruit Trees of America* (1849), a book we had come across at the North family in New Lebanon. In the section on summer apples was a description of the Early Strawberry Apple "erroneously called Red Juneating" which applied, in every detail, to the ones we had picked:

> A beautiful variety which is said to have originated in the neighborhood of New York, and appears in the markets there from July till September. Its sprightly flavour, agreeable perfume, and fine appearance, place it among the very finest summer apples.

The fruit is "roundish," Downing wrote, "narrowing towards the eye"; the skin is "finely striped and stained with bright and dark red, on a yellowish white ground; the flesh white, slightly tinged with red next the skin, tender, sub-acid, and very sprightly and brisk in flavour, with an agreeable aroma."

If further proof were needed, it would have been provided by the wonderful applesauce which Faith has made from these apples, tangy and "brisk in flavour, with an agreeable aroma." Surely this must have been one of the varieties from which the famous Shaker applesauce was made!

THE GIFT TO BE FREE

Richmond, August 1957

Today we had callers from Music Inn in Lenox, a man and his wife who had once lived at the Shaker Mill, or West family in New Lebanon, and while there had acquired a few pieces of Shaker furniture. One of the first remarks he made as he stepped across the threshold and looked around was: "What impresses me about Shaker furniture is that every piece expresses, subtly but unmistakably, the individuality of its maker."

He was right. Though the craftsmanship of the sect was communal in organization and use, there was nothing stereotyped about it. No two pieces, not even chairs, are exactly alike. The joiner's approach was that of an artist, and the finished product reflected his care.

His remark recalled a statement once made by a fine Shaker

craftsman, Elder Hervey L. Eads of the South Union society in Kentucky. His book, *Shaker Sermons: Scripto-Rational Containing the Substance of Shaker Theology,* was in answer to a criticism that the authority of the Shaker elders is "the entire control of the individual under him, body, soul, and mind." Eads wrote:

> The Elder's rule, over the subject's mind, extends no farther than to determine the kind of business he or she is to pursue for the time being, for the benefit of themselves and the community. I will illustrate by my own experience. I was requested in times past to work at various branches of business, mechanical and otherwise, and thereby learned several trades, in all of which I had the freest possible exercise of all my faculties to develop my mechanical genius; my mind was entirely untrammeled by the elder's mind, and was brought as fully and freely into exercise as if I had appointed myself to the several callings.

Further on he said:

> It is the duty of every person on earth to follow any light, or copy any example above them, and there is (no) bondage in so doing. . . . The fact is, the true-souled and obedient Shaker is the freest person on the foot-stool of God, because all his bonds are self-imposed.

The Shaker craftsman was directed by his overseers as he would have been by a responsible father or mother. But once his apprenticeship was served, he was free to express himself and his faith in the medium of wood, metal or words.

In the words of an early Shaker song,

> Tis the gift to be simple
> Tis the gift to be free
> Tis the gift to come down
> Where we ought to be . . . .

A LINK WITH THE PAST

Summer 1963

With one or two exceptions our former Shaker friends, the sisters and brethren we knew intimately, are now gone. And because we do not see them any more, or visit the places where they lived, the past of which they were a part seems strangely removed. It is as if this flowering period of our Shaker adventure were another world, and the culture itself extinct—even though a few members of the order still remain. But out of that other world, one day two years ago, a person appeared who revived, for a short time at least, the feeling that we still belonged to that world.

When she lived at Hancock, from childhood years until 1935, we knew Sister Olive Hayden slightly. There were only a few sisters left then in the community, and only one brother. Its end in sight, Olive felt that her usefulness, more limited every day, did not justify her remaining there. She advertised for a position as a housekeeper or companion, and in the course of time assumed such a responsibility in the home of a widower with children. Later she was married to him.

Her return to Hancock, when she learned it was being restored, was an event: in part, a large part, because she was such a lovely personality, soft-spoken, quiet, observant, intelligent; and in part because she was a rich source of information about the village where she had spent all her early life. She had known all the Hancock Shakers in the post-1903 era, and had anecdotes to tell about many of them. She knew the layout of buildings that had since been razed. She remembered a number of early Shaker songs, and willingly sang them for us.

Her first wish was to revisit the retiring room—No. 12 on the second floor of the brick dwelling—which was hers for so long. And as she went from room to room, and building to building, associations crowded into her mind. The years of absence seemed not to have dimmed her memory, even of details. Her spirit soared. At heart she was a Shakeress again.

In the course of repeated visits she revitalized our sense of time and place. We learned the location of the corn-drying kiln, the boys' shop, the shop where Louis Basting made his table swifts, the identity of the ministry wash house, the use of certain rooms in the machine shop. She knew Emily Curtis and Sophia Helfrich, the last cloak makers at Hancock. She recalled where the coffins were kept, and how the children used to hide in them; and the place where she secreted her forbidden doll. On a visit to the brethren's shop, she not only remembered where Brother Henry Hollister had his work room, but also one of his favorite songs, "The gospel is a treasure." He was stone deaf at the time, but he sang it in a strong tenor voice, eyes shut, and patting his knee to keep time:

> The gospel is a treasure
> That's worth our whole attention
> It brings us low
> By this we know
> It was not man's invention.
>
> 'Twas Jesus the Anointed
> Who first revealed the plan
> And now it is renewed again
> By our good Mother Ann.

When Olive left the Shakers she took with her several chairs and other keepsakes, including a water-color of the Church family done by an unknown artist in 1830. It is probably the earliest pictorial record of the village, a valuable document showing the courtyard east of the family dwelling surrounded by buildings no longer standing. These reminders of her life in the order are precious to her. Her presence at the village, and later in our home, where Faith gave her one of her costumed dolls, was precious to us. For through the purity of her spirit and a dedication that had never been lost our own faith in the Shaker ideal was renewed.

THE AMERICAN MUSEUM IN BRITAIN

It is gratifying to learn that work in which one believes has found a response in other people's minds and in other localities. There was a time when the only value placed on Shaker furniture was its value in the antiques market. For a long time there was no sign of interest in the Shakers in our home town, Pittsfield, or indeed the whole local area. They were usually dismissed as "peculiar people," with no contributions worth consideration. When, for example, we once appealed to certain parties to help us save the Hancock meeting house, we encountered only indifference. When we held our first exhibition, at a well-known antiquarian society in Boston, we were offered a nominal sum for the entire contents of the room! And when we inquired about an exhibit at an important museum in New York, we were told that Shaker crafts-manship was too plain, too ordinary, not worthy of a showing. At one time our work seemed to have come to a dead end.

Then, as we have elsewhere related, the truth began to dawn that though the craftsmanship was deceptively "simple," it was in reality, in its understanding and control of form, sophisticated—"elegant" was Juliana Force's word for it.

Recognition had to come first from the outside. Craftsmen in the Scandinavian countries had recognized its merit before it was generally appreciated in this country: *Shaker Furniture* was well known in the folk museums there. Inquiries began to trickle in from other non-local sources, and when publicity spread in the wake of exhibits there was talk, in certain quarters, of installing Shaker rooms. The culmination of this growing interest was the invitation to install one or more rooms in the American Museum in Britain, near Bath, England.

It had been a common assumption, in that country and on the continent, that America had always borrowed from Europe, that there was little that was truly indigenous in its arts, that its culture was on the whole crass, materialistic, rootless. The American Museum in Britain, founded in 1960, was designed to correct such a fallacy, to demonstrate, in its period rooms and other exhibits, that there did exist in America, traditions of native craftsmanship and distinctive folk and decorative arts.

The opportunity to play a part in this mission was a vindication, as it were, of our faith in the merit of Shaker art. The sponsors of the museum ~~~~~~~~~ ~~ New Haven, and together we selected five repr~~~~~~~~~~~~~~ ~~~niture, household accessories, costumes, sh~~~~~~~~~~~~~~~~ ~~strative of Shaker industry, and docu~~~~~~~~~~~~~~~~~ ~~emorial to Homer Keyes, we gave the ~~~~~~~~~~~~~~~~~ date, of *The Magazine Antiques*. The ~~~~~~~~~~~~~~~ o Claverton, England, to supervise the

~~~~~~~~~~ orable one—not only because the result ~~~~~~~~~ use there was respect everywhere for us ~~~~~~~~ he Shakers, who originally came from ~~~~~~~~ in their own homeland. Nearly two ~~~~~~~ d her little band of followers left the ~~~~~~~ ecuted, to seek freedom of worship in ~~~~~~~ the movement she started its belated

Our Mission

Goodwill changes lives
by helping people
with disabilities or disadvantages
go to work

Tacoma Goodwill Industries
Port Angeles Store
603 South Lincoln
Port Angeles, WA 98362
360.452.2440
Manager Dianna

Sales Receipt

Transaction #:   1242490
Date: 10/28/2011   Time: 12:45:20 PM
Cashier: CANDACE   Register #: 2

                                      Amount
              Description
Item $1.00
15   Books

XXIII

THOMAS MERTON AND THE SHAKERS

One of the great rewards of writing and lecturing is the formation of friendships. After an article or book is published we receive letters from many sources, often followed by visits to our home. Similarly, the talks given at Winterthur, Williamsburg, Dearborn, Smith College, Pleasant Hill and elsewhere have provided opportunities to become acquainted with people who had become interested in the Shakers. The circle constantly widens. Our lives are increasingly enriched.

Of all the people we have come to know as a result of our work none is closer to us in spirit than Thomas Merton (Father Louis) of the Abbey of Gethsemane, Trappist, Kentucky. We knew his book, *The Seven Storey Mountain,* and a mutual friend, Mark Van Doren, had often spoken of him. We had heard that he and Shirley Burden, a photographer, had discussed the possibility of a book on the Shakers. The Cistercian Order had the same ideals of simplicity and good work as the Believers. We longed to know him, and finally wrote him, offering assistance on the book project.

On December 12, 1960, we received a reply. He had two of our studies, *Shaker Furniture* and *The People Called Shakers.* He was grateful for our letter, which had inspired him to pursue his studies further. He had indeed thought of doing a book, not on their doctrines as such, but on "their spirit and I might say their mysticism, in practice, as evidenced by their life and their craftsmanship." He wrote:

> To me the Shakers are of very great significance, besides being something of a mystery, by their wonderful integration of the spiritual and the physical in their work. There is no question in my mind that one of the finest and most genuine religious expressions of the nineteenth century is in the silent eloquence of Shaker craftsmanship.

With humility he inquired if we had "any interesting books that are not too precious to lend," or any reproductions of our Shaker inspirationals. He did not intend to rush at the study he had in mind:

It would be a crime to treat them superficially, and without the deepest love, reverence and understanding. There can be so much meaning to a study of this kind: meaning for twentieth century America which has lost so much in the last hundred years —lost while seeming to gain. I think the extinction of the Shakers and of their particular kind of spirit is an awful portent.

The letter closed with a prayer of blessing on our work.

An opportunity to visit the Abbey and meet Father Thomas presented itself the following year. Plans were under way, on the part of a group of interested citizens to take up the privately held options on the Pleasant Hill property with a view to restoring that lovely community. The group had established an office in Lexington, appointed a director, and initiated a fund raising campaign. a conference was set for Saturday, November 4, 1961, to include a seminar and tour of the village. We were invited, and so was Thomas Merton.

In a letter to the director of the Project, the Trappist wrote that he would not be able to attend, explaining that the monks were not supposed to speak before an audience outside of the monastery. However, he subsequently invited us to visit the Abbey as his guest, and went on to discuss the importance of preserving the Shaker heritage:

The Shakers and their spirituality seem to me to be extremely significant, as an authentic form of the Monastic Life, with a Utopian and eschatological cast. The superb and simple products of their craftsmanship are not only eloquent in themselves, but they also speak for the genuine spiritual vitality of the Shakers, and testify to the energy of their ideal. I believe that much is to be done in the study of the Shaker spirituality in the light of Western and Near Eastern mystical traditions, and also in the light of Jungian depth psychology. Doctrines which were certainly heterodox from a traditional Christian viewpoint, may then assume a special significance in the history of our time. I cannot help feeling that the Shaker movement is something of a mystery that withholds from us, still, a deep significance which may even throw some light on our present predicament in the world, I think this can be said for all the Utopian movements of the nineteenth century, but is especially true of the Shakers. I have as yet no way of substantiating this intuition. Perhaps some day research and scholarship may help us see more clearly into the problem. . . . Certainly these honest and noble people manifested a very sincere desire to seek the highest truth by the means that they thought most adequate for the purpose. They felt that it was necessary to dedicate their lives completely to their ideal, and they did so without reserve. At a time like the present when we are witnessing the moral disintegration of our society under the pressure of enormous and perhaps demonic forces of the mind, we can ill afford to despise the simplicity and dedication to truth of these good sincere people who lived up to their belief.

The visit to the Trappist monastery was a memorable one. At Father Merton's suggestion we arrived in time to attend the short choral office of Nones which was chanted at 1:15 in the afternoon. We met the good brother in a room reserved for visitors, and then he took me on a tour of the Abbey. (The rules forbade Faith from accompanying us.) Though the monastic rule of silence prevailed, in his role as guide and director of novices he was permitted to speak, answering all questions most graciously and with deep insight into the dedicated work of the order. In the book store we selected a volume we wanted to buy—*God is My Life,* with photographs of Gethsemane by Shirley Burden and a forward by Thomas Merton—but he insisted on presenting it to us. "You can buy books elsewhere," he said, "but not here." Nor would he take money for the famed Trappist cheese, so Faith put the money in the poor box. After an hour or so of the best of good talk, we took our leave, gently waved away by one whom we had already come to regard as a spiritual mentor and intimate friend.

Soon afterwards, on December 21, Father Merton wrote us expressing his appreciation for a book we had sent him for the novitiate library:

> I believe it is of the highest importance for the novices to see these things and get used to this wonderful simplicity. This wordless simplicity, in which the works of quiet and holy people speak humbly for themselves. How important that is in our day when we are flooded with a tidal wave of meaningless words: and worse still when in the void of those words the sinister power of hatred and destruction is at work. The Shakers remain as witnesses to the fact that only humility keeps man in communion with truth, and first of all with his own inner truth. This one must know without knowing it, as they did. For as soon as a man becomes aware of "his truth" he lets go of it and embraces an illusion.

Intensely interested in all types of monasticism, Father Merton in the above letter recommended to our curiosity "a very intriguing book," *De Therapeutis,* by Philo Judaeus, the Jewish Platonist who lived in Alexandria. In this book Philo speaks of the Jewish monastic communities in Egypt which, Father Merton noted, had similarities with the Shakers: "They were contemplative communities of men and women, living separately and joining in worship, though separated by a partition."

The next letter in my Merton file is a copy of one he wrote on January 27, 1962, to Mary Black, director of the Abby Aldrich Rockefeller Folk Art Collection at Williamsburg, who had invited him to an exhibition of Shaker spiritual drawings. As in the earlier letter, after expressing his regrets that he could not attend, he added "a few thoughts that are at work in my mind about the Shakers and their deep significance, which manifests itself in a hidden and archetypal way in their art, craftsmanship and in all their works." He went on to explain:

> Their spirit is perhaps the most authentic expression of the primitive American "mystery" or "myth": the paradise myth. The New World, the World of renewal, of return to simplicity, to the innocence of Adam, the recovery of the primeval cosmic simplicity, the reduction of diversions, the restoration of unity. But not just a return to the beginning, it is also an anticipation of the end. The anticipation of eschatological fulfillment, of completion, the New World was an earnest and a type of the New Spiritual creation.

He continued:

> In the secular realm this consciousness was of course very pronounced, the consciousness of the pioneer and later of the business man who thought that America could literally be the earthly paradise. The belief that there was nothing impossible, that all goodness and all happiness were there for the asking. And in the poor of other lands, America existed as the place where they thought gold could be picked up in the streets.
>
> It was a different consciousness, [for the Shakers, however,] for at the same time they saw the deceptiveness of the secular hope, and their eyes were open, in childlike innocence, to the evil, the violence, the unscrupulousness that too often underlie the secular vision of the earthly paradise. It was a paradise in which the Indian had been slaughtered, and the Negro was enslaved. In which the immigrant was treated as an inferior being, and in which he had to work very hard for the "gold" that was to be "picked up in the streets."

The Shakers were conscious of the deceptions in "the earthly paradise," Father Merton felt, and transformed this paradise myth into a special reality.

> [They] realized that to enter into a genuine contract with the reality of the "paradise spirit" which existed in the wonderful new world, they had to undergo a special kind of conversion. And their conversion had this special, unique, wonderful quality in that it, more than any other "spirit," grasped the unique substance of the American paradise myth, and embodied it in a wonderful expression. For myths are realities, and they themselves open into deeper realms. The Shakers apprehended something totally original about the spirit and vocation of America. This has remained hidden to everyone else. The sobering thing is that their vision was—eschatological! And they themselves ended.

There were other letters, about Pleasant Hill, about a monograph I was doing on "Sheeler and the Shakers," about a picture book he hoped to do on the Shakers. He sent us many of his works and recently a beautiful poem, "Grace's House," based on a child's drawing, which he thought would fit the Shirley meeting-house (which had been moved to Hancock) in some "mysterious" way.

One song in *The Gift to be Simple*, "Decisive Work," particularly appealed to him:

> I have come,
> And I've not come in vain.
> I have come to sweep
> The house of the Lord
> Clean, clean, for I've come
> And I've not come in vain.
> With my broom in my hand,
> With my fan and my flail,
> This work I will do
> And I will not fail,
> For lo!   I have come
> And I've not come in vain.

> Sung by the Saviour and Mother Ann.
> Sat. eve. Feby 21st 1845.

The notation was not included in *The Gift,* so I sent it to Father Thomas. He replied:

Dear Edward:

I was touched at your thoughtfulness in sending me the music for the song "Decisive Work." It is what I would have expected, and I have learned it now, so that I can sing it to myself from time to time when I am alone. I am still deeply convinced that it represents a most important insight into our own time. And of course it is for us in our own way by our faith and obedience to all of God's "words" to attune ourselves to His will and to join in His work, according to our own humble capacities. The Shakers saw this so well, and saw that their work was a cooperation in the same will that framed and governs the cosmos: and more, governs history. . . .

With cordial wishes to you both for the New Year, in all friendship, in Christ,

Tom Merton

XXIV

THE SHAKERS AND LAURA LANGFORD

Shaker correspondence was limited to the exchange of letters between members of the ministry and eldership, copies of which were ordinarily retained for the record.* Common members could write letters to and receive them from relatives, but these were carefully censored and the practice was not encouraged. Separation from the world was a cardinal doctrine and all contacts, whether in person or in writing, were kept to a minimum.

However, there were exceptions to the rule. Some family leaders were more liberal than others. In the novitiate orders, where ties with the world were not severed, there was much coming and going. It was to these orders that serious inquiries were directed, and often friendships resulted. Such was the case with Eldress Anna White, of the North family or "gathering order" at Mount Lebanon and Mrs. Laura Holloway Langford. Mrs. Langford had purchased the property of the Upper Canaan, N.Y. Shakers in 1906, which was a branch of the Mount Lebanon North family. Eldress Anna's letters—given to us by a later owner of Upper Canaan—began in 1874, when her correspondent was still Mrs. Holloway. The last letter in the file is dated April 14, 1909.

Laura Langford was a southern woman, whose early life was "passed in affluence amid the cultivated society of the wealthy planters of Tennessee." After the disruptions of the Civil War, she moved to Washington, D.C., where as a guest of President Andrew Johnson for several months, she gathered the material for her best known book, *The Ladies of the White House*. From there she went to Brooklyn,

---

* Once we found, in a disused cupboard at Hancock, a cache of original letters, and copies of letters, exchanged between the eastern and western ministries dating from the earliest establishment of the communities in Kentucky and Ohio.

where for fourteen years she was associated with *The Brooklyn Eagle,* working her way up to a responsible position on the editorial staff. Besides editorials for this paper and the *New York Sun,* she wrote several books and articles; lectured extensively; and edited a magazine of "home literature," *The Lady's World.* Her interests were broad including journalism, literature, social reform, theosophy and mysticism. She was a close friend of Madame Blavatsky. In London she was associated in the publication of a book *Mysticism in the East.* She was president of The Leidl Society, whose purpose was to give working girls, and "women with children and without escort," an opportunity to enjoy good music at nominal prices.

It is understandable how, with such interests, an acquaintance would eventually be formed with a neighbor who was one of the most progressive leaders of the Shaker society. The correspondence is enlightening on many counts, not the least of which was Eldress Anna's dependence on her worldly friend for advice on matters with which the Shakeress had little experience.

In the 1874 letter, the first eldress of the North family, Antoinette Doolittle, welcomes Laura, who had been abroad, to her "home and friends in America." Then Anna, a practical person as well as a spiritual leader, after adding her own greeting, attends to business:

> We shall not have sufficient apples for our own use, and consequently cannot meet your request for them. Of potatoes we have an abundance and are claimed to be superior. We sell them for 50¢ a bushel. We can also supply you with butter, that we sell at 30¢ a lb. We lay that down in 10 and 19 lb. tubs. You would likely want the butter sent by express, and the potatoes as freight.

In subsequent letters Eldress Anna confides her problems and seeks advice on many matters. Laura had recommended a boy—Charlie—to the North family hoping he would "grow steady and industrious and become a good, useful man" but the experiment wasn't succeeding. There was "no fun, no games, no nothing," the boy complained. "The change from the excitement of city life to the quiet stillness of country life," Anna wrote, "we fear is too great a change . . . He is making trouble by walking off and no one knowing where he is, and says he . . . does not want to be a Shaker."

When the communities at Mount Lebanon and Watervliet were about to apply to the legislature for exemption from taxation—on the grounds that they were a religious institution, and had also served the state "in the unaided care, protection and education provided to friendless children and youth and their other charitable work"—Anna wrote to Laura (July 15, 1903) for advice as to the best method of procedure.

The following year she sought counsel again, this time on the manuscript of *Shakerism: Its Meaning and Message,* on which she was then working in collaboration with Leila Taylor. She had requested Funk & Wagnalls to send the manuscript to Mrs. Langford.

> If you can help us to a better publisher, and advise us as to terms and stipulations we shall be greatly your debtors, as we have had but little experience with publishers. . . . Any changes, omissions or additions that you might suggest we should gratefully accept and consider.

Anna's letters to Laura are a running record of events during the first decade of the present century. On April 18, 1904 she reports the sale of Shaker property in Canaan, N.Y. to the Berkshire Industrial Farm. It was offered at a great sacrifice financially:

"We are glad to do it, however, and shall be glad if we can feel that the consecrated soil is being employed to better human conditions and uplift tempted youth to noble manhood."

The Shakers always celebrated the anniversary of Mother Ann Lee's arrival in America on August 6th. On the last day of July, in 1904, Eldress Anna again seeks advice on "what arrangements to make, what arrangements you have made, how many you have, or are going to invite, etc". She is anxious to have J.P. MacLean, one of the speakers, meet Laura, and asks if the Shakers could use Laura's name "in publishing for Mother's meeting." Other matters also concern her. She asks about a certain Swede and his mother whom Laura had mentioned as being interested in coming to Mount Lebanon. She writes:

> The North family could put them up in an empty house in the village, the "Mt. Lebanon home." He could work for us—for the brothers—and she could help us start a business that the sisters could carry on—confectionary . . . . We want to engage in something else than the making of cloaks. The hand sewing, which is the part we do, is ruinous to the eye sight.

A letter written in November, 1904, was in response to one of Laura's asking about the Shakers' experience with "spirit return," and particularly about the case of Sister Annie Byrdsall. Anna feels free to tell her friend of her own experience with this lately deceased member of the family:

> Looking out one morning from our shop window upon the lawn opposite, her [Annie Byrdsall's] favorite resort, with never a thought of her, a shock as of electricity passed thro' me as I saw her for an instant in the same attitude as we had so often seen her a few weeks since when in the body. It was as quick as a flash and all was over.

Eldress Anna seemed undecided about the authenticity of such "manifestations." The Byrdsall experience, she wrote, was not materialization "nor hardly clairvoyance." She hesitated even to relate

Laura Langford

Eldress Anna White

Eldress Antoinette Doolittle

it. She had decided to leave out of her new book the Shakers' experience with the well-known spiritualist William Eddy.

As usual, the letter discourses on many subjects. Anna refers to Laura's booklet, *The Story of a Piano*—the only Langford publication with Shaker subject-matter—saying that it was "beautifully told and will have ready sale (though) it may possibly mislead people to think we are more liberal than is really the case." She then discussed crops and the weather; the response, on the part of the Berkshire Athenaeum in Pittsfield—which had (quite) a collection of Shaker literature—to the circular announcing *Shakerism: Its Meaning and Message;* the state of people's health; a possible exhibit in Brooklyn of "things remaining in store for sale," and so on.

The great event in 1905 was the peace convention organized by Eldress Anna, Eldress Leila Taylor and others at the North family. Previous to the two day affair starting August 31, Anna's letters were filled with details of arrangements and questions regarding certain speakers. "We are becoming popular," she writes on August 22, "and popularity is dangerous in one sense, it puffs up, in the other it works like leaven, inspiring to do more, urging on to greater efforts for the betterment of the world."

Anna's last letter in our file, written on a dark, rainy morning in April, 1909, sums up the meaningful relationship between the two women:

> Thank you for . . . the deep interest you take in our welfare. You are our Aaron—our mouth-piece. You do more in defence of the cause than we can, in one way. Some will read and believe what an outsider says where it would be useless for us to combat.

Laura Langford had endeared herself not only to Anna White but to other New Lebanon Shakers who had corresponded with her about matters both spiritual and temporal. After her death in 1930, letters were found from Leila Taylor, Elder Daniel Offord, Elder Frederick Evans, Emma and Sadie Neale, Catherine Allen, Martha Burger and William Anderson. (Elder William went into detail on the pedigree of a Guernsey bull that Laura had bought.) Altogether they give an interesting insight into the day-to-day affairs of a busy Shaker family adjusting itself to declining membership and changing times. Though courage never wavers, the insights are often depressing. That these people who had separated from the world and confidently expected to build "a new earth" eventually came to depend, as in this case, on succor from the world, has its overtones of pathos. It is sad to witness the decline of a culture.

XXV

SHAKER FARM

July 1950

Though our dream of saving a community, or even one Shaker house has never come true, we have had great satisfaction in restoring an old New England farmhouse in the Shaker manner.

We had long wanted a place in the country, preferably in Richmond, Massachusetts, a village of scattered farms pleasantly situated in a narrow valley between the Taconic and Lenox mountain ranges. There had been Andrewses in Richmond since 1781, when Ozias Andrews, yeoman, brought his wife, Anna Knott, and their children by ox-cart from Southington, Connecticut. My paternal great grandfather, Selah Andrews, a "spoon smith," had a farm there. In Sleepy Hollow, below the meeting house, my grandfather was born. And on a rocky hill farm in another part of the town, a great aunt, Elvira Andrews, once raised sheep, tending them alone until she died at a ripe old age. As a boy on this farm, I learned the ways of the country—in the hay fields, cow barns and vegetable gardens.

Richmond was full of memories, the product of both inheritance and experience. When we were married, it was the place we naturally chose for a honeymoon. Later, when our children were growing up, we used to take them at every opportunity for picnics on a secluded slope beside Cone Brook, a little stream that meanders through the valley. We went for outings to other places in the Berkshires—Stockbridge Bowl, Wahconah Falls in Dalton and Disappearing Brook in Lanesboro—but we always returned to Richmond, drawn by an irresistible force. We wanted it to be home.

Compulsion waxed so strong that in the middle thirties we began to look for a place there. Sleepy Hollow and the sheep farm were in other hands as well as an old house which had once been the poor house on Dublin Road. (The road, a seldom used byway winding through the center of town, had once been called Town Farm Cross Road, but had been renamed Dublin after the Irish immigrants who used to work in the Richmond iron mines.) We loved the old road, though, and on our drives to Cone Brook, usually took that route, casting envious glances at the poor house and admiring the ancient umbrella elm which grew beside the road a short distance to the north. Delegation of the search to a farm agency was unsuccessful.

Then one day, stopping by the old elm, we noticed that behind a lilac bush, and all but concealed by shrubbery, gnarled apple trees and two maples, was a dilapidated salt box farm house, its chimney crumbling, its shingles rotting away, its window panes cracked or missing, its sides covered with tar paper where the clapboards had fallen off. The dooryard was littered with rubbish. The remains of auto bodies lay scattered about the orchard. A large barn with a sagging ridgepole, near which were two sheds about to collapse, loomed in the background. The place was deserted.

It must have been a measure of our desperation that we investigated the place at all. But we peered through the windows, and not being discouraged even then, obtained the key from the owner down the road. It was for sale, he said, for the last occupant had recently abandoned it as a place unfit for habitation. And well he might, for the interior proved to be worse than the outside: two floors had caved in; the walls and wallpaper (newspaper glued on) were streaked with dirt, soot and rust; the sills were rotten; the cellar stairs were gone; and an old stove sagged, with one leg missing, in a corner of the "living room." The second story was no better: most of the floor boards were missing, and overhead the protruding shingle nails made it hazardous to stand erect. Tin cans, bottles and old clothes were strewn about everywhere.

There was something about the house, though, that appealed to us. We suspected that behind the lath-and-plaster ceiling there were sturdy beams The chair rail, the windows that retained their original sash and glass, the glimpses of old sheathing, all gave hints of former splendor. The elm, the lilac bushes, the two maples standing guard by the front door, these had given us pause. The way the house nestled beside the road had won our hearts. With all its disrepair, it stood foursquare, structurally sound, with something of the pride of a fine old gentleman fallen on evil days.

We bought it in faith but in trepidation. Perhaps "bought it" is not the right phrase, for the small sum we paid—the first royalty on our furniture book—represented only the value of the land, the ten acres of rolling meadow and a small wood lot. Then, little by little, summer by summer, we restored it. Sills, clapboards, shingles and chimney first. Outside, two coats of Indian red paint—no trim. Inside, with the help of a country carpenter, we ripped off the ceiling lath uncovering (besides corn cobs, squirrel nests, rags and papers) the stout beams which tied the house together. An English mason rough-plastered the

Before Restoration
In November, 1937, we purchased our farm house and 10 acres in Richmond, as photographed by our son David at age 14. Proudly we posted the "No Trespassing" sign and left for our winter's work.

After Restoration
Shaker Farm—the dream had come true.

walls, which we painted flat white. Walter Salmon, our carpenter, replaced the ugly front door with a batten door from the Shakers, and one upstairs with a paneled door from the same source, in both cases using Shaker hand-wrought latches and hinges. The fireplace was gone, but we had Shaker stoves, and the original hearth stone, uncovered in the cellar mud, became our front door step.

So much to do, but so much fun. The house responded like a living being, growing more beautiful every day. The interior wood-work was painted the green-blue of the Shaker meeting rooms in Kentucky, the floors "Shaker red" or mustard yellow. The bedrooms upstairs were cellotexed and painted white, except for the old timbers; missing floor boards were replaced by wide pine boards from the partition of a Shaker shop. Then came the time when we set up the Shaker stove and moved furniture in. The transformation was complete. All was clean, orderly and colorful. And oh, the peace, the quiet of the countryside!

Much, of course, remained to be done: practical things like drilling a well, moving an outhouse, installing a telephone, tearing down a pig-pen and carriage shed, making the cow barn over into a combination study and dormitory; and pleasurable projects like kitchen and herb gardening. In planting two rows of lilac bushes by our front door in memory of Mr. and Mrs. Keyes we were following a tradition, for we later learned that the two maples had been planted by a former owner as a memorial to two sons lost in a war.

Once settled, we delved into the history of the house, learning that it had been built about 1795 by a certain Daniel Hand, a weaver, who came to Richmond from New Lebanon. Of its many owners, one, to our surprise, was Truman Bishop Andrews, an ancestor, who brought his bride here just one hundred years before we took title.

So much has happened at Shaker Farm that it seems as if it has been our lifetime home. The children, then in their teens, found it lonesome at first. They were isolated from their friends, they felt, with little to do—no radio, no electric light to read by in the evening. Rising earlier than was their wont, they had to walk a mile or more to take the bus to school. In time, though, their attitude changed. Friends came to them. Ann went off to college, David into the service, and when they returned, they began increasingly to share our affection for the place. First one, then the other married and honeymooned there, and now they bring *their* children here. Teddy II, David's oldest, was washed in the old stone sink and rinsed under the pump before his christening. Now he and his brothers, Gary and Peter, exult in the open spaces that don't exist in their part of Westchester. For Ann and her two children, Linda and Jeffrey, Shaker Farm is also the family homestead, one that is rich in memories of good times.

We all love the seclusion, the changing seasons, the country people. One farmer plants his oats, corn and potatoes on the land across the road. Another has the use of our land, which was fast going to weeds and brush, and reaps from it bountiful harvests of wheat, barley and hay. The land responds to care. Birds sing all day long. The troubles of the world seem far away.

It would not have been right, however, to keep the world away. Nor did we want to. Friends were welcome as were visitors interested in the Shakers. The farm has been photographed four times: by the *Christian Science Monitor, The Magazine Antiques,* Harper's *Junior Bazaar* and *Ladies Home Journal.* The *Monitor* pictures gave the rooms a stark quality; we were such purists at first that, Shaker-wise, we had no pictures on the walls. In *Antiques* they look more liveable without losing their monastic appearance. The *Bazaar* and *Journal* worked in color, the former using furniture as backdrops for models dressed in a fashion line inspired by Shaker costume. Ezra Stoller's assignment for the *Journal* posed at first a problem. After he had unloaded his equipment on a dark, rainy day he discovered that "the primitive appearance of the house and its furnishings, so pure and simple and period-perfect, was authentic to the point that when he began looking up connections for his battery of powerful floodlights, it turned out the nearest electricity was a quarter of a mile away!" "Fortunately," the editor of the *Journal* continued, "he'd come prepared for most emergencies, and the color was shot with flash equipment; taking a lot more time and trouble, but rather fitting in view of the time and trouble the Shakers had taken. The results, which may be seen in the March, 1950, issue of the *Journal* and in Richard Pratt's *Second Treasury of Early American Homes,* were all that could be desired. The rooms looked lived in. They looked Shaker. They looked proud and happy.

The present chapter is written on a Shaker starch table in the refurbished barn room. It is a cool sunny morning late in July. As the writer looks out the open door he can see the branches of the "Seek-no-further" apple tree waving gently in the breeze, and beyond Farmer Malnati and his sons mowing their wheat. Little Linda is playing under the maples, and as she softly chatters a song sparrow sings a sweet refrain.

Homer Keyes was right. "Here there is peace. Here one can be oneself."

XXVI

PROBLEMS IN COLLECTING

All collectors are faced with the problems involved in buying, installing, preserving and so on. Some are solvable; others elude satisfactory solution. Our problems were not essentially different from those of other persons interested and increasingly immersed in some given field. We hope we are not numbered among those whose collections own *them*, and who must have moments when they think, "Blessed be nothing!"

In one respect, however, we believe our experience has been unusual. As Gladys A. Reichard once pointed out, in a review in the *Journal of American Folk Lore,* collectors generally gather together material objects with intensity and then "set them apart as if they were isolated from all other aspects of life." If there is any documentation at all it seldom goes beyond "mere diagram and description." But these material objects, Miss Reichard contended, are "more than things, more than mere items for the adornment of the musty rooms of museums"; and since they were once "closely coordinated with the social, religious, economic and psychological background of their owners, they can be fully appreciated only in terms of the way of life of which they were an expression."

There is a difference, so it seems to us, between the person who merely accumulates objects *per se* and the one who sees them in the perspective of social history or use. As his interest develops, the true collector is presented with opportunities which give that interest ever widening dimensions. In seeking thus to give his collection the fullest meaning possible, decisions of many kinds have to be made. These *are* problems.

Some of them are minor. We have gotten used to repeating the story of how we became engaged in what people thought was a very unorthodox pursuit. We are patient when people ask us if we ourselves are Shakers. We try to explain, without much success, why the Shakers adopted the principle of celibacy, and what would become of the world if all became Shakers. They can comprehend Catholic but not Shaker monasticism.

Answering letters is a tax on one's time, but not really a major problem either. We could let them go unanswered, because, as is generally the case, no stamps or self-addressed envelopes are enclosed. We were surprised, at first, however, by the fact that so few were thoughtful inquiries about the sect, or contributions in any way to our knowledge.

What then, do people write about? Chairs mostly. The society sold chairs to the world as early as the 1790's and, in quantity, after the Philadelphia Centennial of 1876. After the latter date a patent was obtained, catalogues were issued, styles were numbered, and a trade-mark affixed to the chairs. Distributors handled the product as far south as Baltimore and as far west as Chicago. Chairs went all over the country. And from near and far we still receive letters with much the same content: "I have a chair which has been in our family for over a hundred years . . . . What is it worth? . . . Will you buy it? . . . Where can I have it re-seated? . . . How should it be refinished? . . . Where and when was it made? . . . Enclosed is a photograph of a chair I recently bought at an auction. Is it Shaker?" (It usually isn't.)

We feel it a duty to answer such letters, though it is not very rewarding, and there is seldom an acknowledgement. We have learned caution, however, and never estimate value: most correspondents think their chair is so rare as to be priceless.

The situation is more complicated when people ask for help on some lecture they're giving, an article they're writing, a student paper, even an exhibition. We are solicited for suggestions, sources of data, answers to involved questions, and the loan of books.

It is well, we have found to be selective. Some "authors" do not even trouble to ask for information. They find it easier to quote phrases, or even whole sentences, from one's books or articles— without using quotation marks. And there have been times when we regretted giving permission. In a case in point, we once tentatively agreed to help with a museum exhibit, but when we invited the curator to our home and found him so insensitive to the beauty of Shaker design, we didn't have the heart to go ahead. After he had gone, Faith went around our living room, touching each piece of furniture, saying, "I feel for you. We'll care for you." (We do get sentimental at times.)

The experience reminds us of an incident in Greenwich Village. We were at a party honoring the poet Robert Frost, whom we had first met years ago when he was at his South Shaftsbury farm in Vermont. (We had gone there to show him some Shaker songs.) At the party a small group had gathered around the distinguished guest, and in the course of the conversation the subject of the Shakers came up. We forget what exactly was said, only that someone made remarks either derogatory or untrue; but we'll not forget what the poet said, in an aside, when the others had moved on: "We know things, don't we?"

In two Shaker families the problem arose as to which of two factions we would work with in our research and collecting. In one family there was a schism between the trustee who held the purse and the authority to sell on a large scale, and the rest of the family, who lived in another dwelling. The family eldress had limited authority, but it was in that family and not in the trustees' office where we had formed our friendships. The situation was somewhat similar in another community whose last two surviving members were sisters by blood as well as by faith. The older of the two was an eldress, but we were closer to the other sister, who held the lower rank of deaconess. Both were trustees with separate domains of authority which they guarded jealously. Again we had to choose and again, the ties of friendship prevailed.

Sometimes the jealousies went deep. One Shaker trustee took a dislike to us for the simple reason that we had the goodwill of a family from whom she had become alienated. No effort on our part could break down her hostility. And she had power and influence, as we learned on one particular occasion. We had collected and paid for a number of items in a dwelling whose occupants were to be moved to another part of the village. As we were carrying a lovely early sewing stand down the stairs, we were confronted by a grim-faced, powerfully built female, arms akimbo, who blocked the passage and ordered us, in the name of the aforementioned trustee, to return it to the place where we had found it.

There was also the person, not a Shaker, but a kind of lord of the manor, who had such a sense of vested interest in the society's property—he had once been its lawyer—that he was outraged when any of that property, in the form of artifacts, was bought by an outsider. Because in a way we were the worst offenders he developed almost a neurosis about us, as if we were thieves. "I could shoot those Andrews," he was heard to remark on one occasion.

It is curious, such resentment or jealousy. We have encountered it continuously, even among people whom we have helped to form collections, but who later disavowed our assistance and became estranged. A national magazine devoted an entire issue to Shaker craftsmanship, using illustrations from our collection, without mentioning the source. A history was written, but the author preferred to keep it secret until it was in print. Illustrations from the furniture book—which was of course copyrighted—seem to others to be in the public domain.

When we wrote *Shaker Furniture: The Craftsmanship of an American Communal Sect,* we felt that reproduction of the furniture in the future might be possible. It was Ananda Coomaraswamy, wiser than we, who challenged our assertion on two counts: that the conditions under which it was first produced would never again prevail, and that it was psychologically impossible to reproduce a given piece exactly.

Experience to date has confirmed his judgment. One of three things happens when a furniture-maker is inspired by Shaker design:

1) He tries to improve on the original
2) He decides to adapt Shaker ideas of function, or simplicity, in order to create a new style
3) He tries to achieve an exact copy

The first practice is the most reprehensible: to put "lappers" or "fingers" on tables, stands and beds, as one designer did, employing a device which the Shakers used only on oval boxes, is to distort without justification what was once reasonable and pure. The "Shaker" line that was foisted on the market in this instance was a sorry sight and deserved its early demise.

The second, adaptation, seems more legitimate, for the designer at least is seeking in the old, "new directions." It is not, however, authentic reproduction.

The third course, like the first, is doomed to aesthetic failure. Currently attempts are being made to copy early forms. Original models, not the best, unfortunately, are available to the workmen. With the aid of calipers, sanders, modern tools, finishes, etc. one might expect faithful adherence to the models. But what happens? Aside from the fact that it is impossible to reproduce the subtle effects of use and age, the copyists take liberties here and there, confident they are improving on the original. The wood may not be well seasoned The marks of the chisel betray the machine. The spray gun is a poor substitute for finish by the careful hand. The finished product—especially if made in quantity to insure a profit—inevitably *looks* like a reproduction.

Every piece of Shaker craftsmanship had its own individuality. It is as if the craft resisted exploitation. As an expression of a religious faith, and painstakingly designed for religious usage, it will not be corrupted.

We once had an amusing experience with one line of reproductions. Samples were being exhibited in the window of a Sixth Avenue shop in New York. Without revealing our identity we engaged the proprietress in talk, and the conversation running to Shaker, she recounted a recent incident. A large man, a sort of Burl Ives, happened along the avenue, gazed for some time at the furniture on display, then thrust his head in the doorway with the remark:

"Its all wrong, all wrong. The celibate Shakers did not believe in reproducing!"

And with that, he walked on.

Solutions to some problems are decided by circumstances pretty much beyond one's control—the question, for example of how comprehensive a collection should be. Once one starts to document a whole culture with artifacts, nothing should be omitted: trivia, materials difficult to preserve like costumes, late as well as early workmanship. For lack of space, however, we had to draw the line at bulky machines, vehicles—and houses. We could have acquired herb presses, trip hammers, dye vats, washing machines, turning lathes, landing stages, and so on, but where would we have stored them? A large cast and wrought iron cooking arch, with the blocks of marble on which it rested, was the heaviest article we ever bought. Vehicles were a temptation which we resisted, though we would have liked to own one of the one-horse wagons which the Shakers "invented," or an ancient hearse from Enfield, Connecticut.

As for houses, we had to be content with removable parts such as pegboards, hardware, built-in cupboards, perhaps a door. One whole day was spent loading into our station wagon the discarded pegboards of an old dwelling being razed at the Upper Canaan (N.Y.) settlement. We almost bought a small shop from Canterbury. We coveted a trim barrel-roofed privy at the North family in New Lebanon, but in this case, too, the problem of transportation was unsolvable.

How we acquired the complete interior of the meeting room of the Hancock church has been told in another chapter. We removed interior parts of the room but the problem was reconstruction. So far, it has served but one purpose—the providing of material for a color photograph in *Life*. We had to be satisfied, in the long run, with architectural drawings and old photographs of buildings, including the stereographs of another day.

In retrospect, all the problems we have recounted seem small when compared with the overshadowing one: what to do with what we had collected. If dispersed, it would never be possible, we knew, to assemble a comparable one, one as selective and comprehensive, one so thoroughly documented.

More attention than ever before is given to conserving our heritage. Old houses—with or without historical associations—are being preserved. Important collections are finding a use in colleges and universities. Regional museums and restorations are springing up everywhere. Local, state and national historical societies are on the increase. A magazine is devoted wholly to the field. Scholars everywhere are engaged in research, and in interpretation and reappraisal of movements, events and personalities. American folk art, music, architecture and religion are receiving unprecedented attention.

Testimonials are not lacking regarding the importance of conserving our own collection. As early as 1930 the secretary of a well-known preservation society wrote us:

> With reference to your own collection in Pittsfield, my feeling is that it would be a national calamity to have this dispersed. . . . Its preservation intact as a monument to the splendid restrained taste and wonderful vitality and perseverance of the Shakers is an objective worthy of the most careful consideration and sustained effort. . . .

And some ten years later the director of a large city museum, appealing for funds from a certain foundation, declared that:

> It is hardly necessary for me to tell you of the importance of the Andrews' contribution to the history of American art. I hope very much that it may be possible for their collection and their work to become a permanent monument to the Shaker tradition.

Sometimes the problem of what to do with our own collection wears a personal aspect. We have become so intimately identified with these things, have lived with them so long and handled them so much—we wonder if we will be moving furniture in heaven!—that to see them go, and perhaps lose their identity, would be like losing part of ourselves. The problem is complicated by the fact that we see the collection in a historical and educational light. It may be a foolish notion, but often, in a mystical mood, we consider ourselves as "instruments" chosen to do a certain work; trustees, as it were, of part of the American heritage. We want to pass it on, intact and unadulterated, to future generations.

XXVII

EXPERIENCES IN DONORSHIP

In the early spring of 1956 representatives of Yale University approached us with an alluring project: that we donate our collection to that institution, remain for a given period as consultant to install, exhibit and catalogue it, and give an experimental course in Yale's new American studies program. Present at the first conference were the dean of the school of architecture and design, the director of the art gallery, and the curator of the university's library of American literature. The project had the enthusiastic endorsement of the chairman of the studies program.

It was alluring for many reasons: the preservation of the collection—intact, the promise of its continuing usefulness as a corpus of historical material, and the opportunity it offered of interpreting this material in an educational environment. No longer would we be concerned about its future, about loss by theft or fire, a forced dispersion of the collection, or the uncertainties attendant on the execution of our estate. A long period of semi-isolation would end with the collection and its donors going out into the active world of scholarship and museum enterprise. The university would be a center for Shaker studies.

We were pleased that our work had been so signally honored. The project was approved in another conference in New Haven attended by the provost. I wrote an article for a national magazine outlining its nature and potentialities.*

The university circulated a press release. I resigned my position in an eastern preparatory school. An inventory was made out describing the collection in detail. Summer and early fall were employed in assembling material from our apartment in Yonkers and our place in the country—furniture, industrial objects, books and photographs, the

---

* "The Shakers in a New World," *The Magazine Antiques,* October, 1957.

structural materials from an early Shaker meeting house. Added to all this was the content of an exhibit which had been on loan for several years at Cooperstown, New York.

The first year of my tenure as "Consultant on Shaker Culture and History" was spent in various ways: preparing a descriptive, interpretative catalogue for an opening exhibition (a considerable sum had been allocated for the publication); cataloguing books, pamphlets and manuscripts for the library; setting up an exhibit in the Sterling Memorial Library; giving talks to students, clubs and the New Haven Colony Historical Society; attending staff meetings and circulating informally in university circles. We made plans for a lecture-concert on Shaker music and explored the possibilities, within the American Studies program, of a Shaker opera in the theater. We had a large room in the art gallery, with an adjoining office, in which selected pieces from the collection were installed. Before the end of the academic year we had transferred some fifteen cartons of books to the university library. In the catalogue for the new year I was listed as giving a course in, of all things, "Problems in American Art." All was in readiness for the exhibition which would herald our bequest.

Then came a series of events which drastically altered the whole situation. A new dean of the school of architecture and design was appointed. The office of the provost changed hands. A new director of the art gallery replaced the incumbent, one whose interests and policy were at variance with those of his predecessor. The chairman of the American studies program took a year's leave of absence, and his duties were delegated to a person with little sympathy for the Shaker project. Death claimed a former secretary of Yale on whom we could have relied for support.

Our gift had been to the university as a whole and accepted by the corporation, but such changes in departmental personnel and policy foredoomed its purposes. The library, we learned, would be distributed to various departments of the institution: the music school, the divinity school, the main library and its branches. We could have our exhibition and publish our catalogue, but after it was over, we were casually told one day, the materials would be consigned to storage, or in the case of the furniture, sent out to furnish masters' houses. Vetoed outright was the original idea of a permanent Shaker exhibit, of one or more appropriately furnished rooms which would serve for seminars and tell the story of the culture. "No space," we were told.

There was nothing to do but withdraw the gift. Everywhere, within and without the college community, were expressions of surprise and disappointment. "Yale's loss," we heard at every turn. An essential university function, we were told, was to build up "a collection of collections," libraries as well as artifacts, and "teaching collections." Collections such as ours which documented communal effort, the work of plain people, were as deserving of study as the production of celebrated artists and artisans. Shaker workmanship, it was pointed out, represented an important strain in the American heritage, serving as a necessary balance to the rare, the exceptional, the high style—it went to the roots of our common life. But this was to no avail. Nor was there any redress.

Our second year was one of disengagement. As the situation became known within the academic circle, there was a noticeable lessening of interest. Someone was heard to say that the collection was "a white elephant." Student applications to take the course were pigeonholed. The collection was put in storage. The books at the library were decatalogued at our request. The year dragged on, an experience in overlordship not dissimilar from the one when we were subjected to federal control.

In fairness to the university it should be stated that the administration was fully aware that *its* commitment had not been fulfilled and that it freely accepted all responsibility. An official letter from the provost terminated, in good faith, what we all had hoped would be a productive pioneer project.

AN INTERIM NOTE

Richmond
July 1957

The experience at Yale served at least one useful purpose, demanding that we organize the industrial material which had accumulated over the years. I find this paper among my notes.

Faith and I have been so busy cleaning, organizing and listing the Shaker industrial objects in the upper barn that today is the first opportunity I have had in some time to add to our memoirs. Neither of us realized how extensive this collection was, nor how difficult it would be to bring order out of chaos. Now, at least, there are aisles, and one can obtain a general idea of categories. A loom, reels, scarns, reeds and weaving paraphernalia are assembled in one corner; baskets are all together; chairs hung from the rafters; benches we put in one place, apple-corers in another, medicinal herb containers in another, patterns and forms in still another, and so on. There are now baskets devoted separately to tinware, ironware and small woodenware. In a dough trough are miscellaneous tools. One large basket holds bolts of cloth; another, dresses. Cots are in a corner, and nearby is a box of wooden bed rollers. Most of the coopersware—dry measures, firkins, spit boxes, pails, etc.—is piled high in a huge adult cradle. Delicate small tools, and collections of spools, chair buttons, labels, kitchen utensils are stored in boxes. An itemized inventory would take months to complete, but we now know in a general way what we've collected. We've made a beginning of a catalogue.

As we lifted, shifted and swept, day after day we heard the excited protests of a mother robin who kept flying about the barn, lighting for a moment on a rafter, a suspended chair, a spinning wheel. We suspected there was a nest of young birds somewhere, but it seemed late in the season for breeding, and the only evidence was the alarmed fluttering about of the parent. Then yesterday I heard, over my head, the hungry "cheep-cheep-cheep" of the brood, and looking up, saw the nest in the seat of a small three-slat chair. Crowded in it were four small birds with beaks wide open.

It was a great relief to have all the industrial artifacts finally organized. The monograph on the Shaker economy had been completed years ago and that added to our sense of accomplishment. These moves represented steps in the right direction, but so much remained.

"PRIVATE PROPERTY. KEEP OUT!"

In 1959, shortly before Shaker Community, Inc., was organized at Hancock, Mass., and before I became its curator, we had occasion to revisit the Church family property there. The three sisters who were the last surviving members had recently moved away, and the property was in charge of a Shaker-appointed caretaker.

On the one occasion when the Shakers wished to exclude the world, they erected high wooden crosses in front of their meeting house and office, inscribed in Biblical language with a plea for privacy.* That was in the days of their prime. On this visit to Hancock there were three quite different signs. One read "Private Property. Keep Out." Another announced an "Overnight Guest House." The third advertised "Land for Sale." Each one was a symbol of a culture in decay.

Why the first sign, nailed to a tree in front of the beautiful brick dwelling? Why "Private Property," a term anathema to the communitarian mind? Why "Keep Out," from a sect which once wanted the world to visit, to trade, to witness the ecstasy of religious dance and song? No one was left in a family which a century ago numbered a hundred. The fifty rooms or more in the dwelling are empty. There were no union meetings, no worship, no children taken in, no work for a cause. The aged sisters who but recently occupied the family dwelling had no energy left to guide the strangers about. They lived in the past. The buildings, too, seemed to live in the past.

Almost as forlorn was the "Guest House," which used to be the

* See Chapter V

197

Trustees office and store. Living there were the caretaker and his family, to whom the Shaker leadership gave the privilege of letting rooms for overnight. The caretaker's wife took us through the building. Room after room was furnished in cheap, garish modern, flowered wallpaper, the last word in utilities. Except for the built-in cupboards, now gaudily painted, not a vestige was left of Shaker craftsmanship—not even a peg board. There was no link with tradition, least of all in the person of the caretaker, who had no knowledge of or feeling for the life which so long pervaded these rooms. The house proclaimed a dead past.

And there was "Land for Sale." For us this was no less tragic than the deserted dwelling and the house relegated to commercial use. For the Shaker leadership, instead of caring for the perpetuation of their heritage, seemed to care now only for profit on land which had originally been consecrated to the service of God. At Hancock, the old meeting-house and a lovely sisters' shop had but recently been torn down—to save taxes, it was said, or the cost of repairs. It was rumored that the lot, standing at the junction of two main arteries of traffic, would be sold for a gas station.

Poignant indeed was the probable fate of this quiet village, which the Shakers called "The City of Peace." The round stone barn, a landmark in the region, was falling apart. Other buildings stood like ghosts, silently chiding an indifferent world for their neglect. No one seemed to care. On Route 20 the world rushed past to outdoor movies, cafes, baseball games. What would the covenanters say, asleep in the burying ground on the slope of their sacred mountain? For a century and a half these Believers in a millennial order labored to make the community a "heaven on earth." For the increase of the gospel they left husbands, wives and children. All they possessed they gave to the Church. They sowed and harvested, worked from dawn to dark and created a home of beauty. Is this scene of desolation and desertion their reward?

Our hearts were wrung. In utter sadness we drove away.

SHAKER COMMUNITY, INC.

A year later, in 1960, a group of interested persons formed Shaker Community, Inc., and the buildings and acreage at Hancock were acquired for the purpose of restoring an entire Shaker settlement. This was the first step in what promised to be a unique project combining an extensive educational program with preservation of cultural values.

As members of this group, our responsibility in the hoped-for restoration was twofold: 1) supervision of the village restoration; and,

2) the gift of our total collection to be installed as the appropriate areas were made ready. In the brochure outlining the aims of Shaker Community, Inc., at Hancock, we had stressed the importance of preserving not only the buildings and artifacts but the spiritual character of the culture. We wanted to conserve *values,* to create a setting which "breathes the spirit of the original culture"—to make the community again a "living organization."

After nearly three years as curator and program consultant of the restoration, I found that this purpose was the most difficult one to achieve. Buildings were being restored. The yards were in Shaker order. Gradually we were installing and documenting materials to tell the story of the Believers' industry, craftsmanship and way of life. Even in this short period the village compared favorably with other outdoor or regional museums. Superficially, the setting bore "the aspect . . . of the original culture," as stated in the original proposal. But that was not enough. What eluded us was the spirit. The village did not breathe; it had no pulse.

This was the most difficult period of our lives and, even today, is painful to chronicle. There was an ever widening gap between the project's direction and our own sense of Shaker values, and it became increasingly difficult to find common ground with the board of trustees. In 1963 we resigned from Shaker Community, Inc., wishing it well and leaving the great majority of our collection which represented the work of a lifetime. A Descriptive Catalogue of this gift to Shaker Community, Inc., follows this chapter.

We felt that in any Shaker restoration the people who operate such a project should be not only versed in its history and tradition, but determined that the intrinsic values of simplicity, humility, cooperation, equality and justice be translated into the life of the institution. More important than all else was that everyone *believe* in the Shaker legacy and, in so doing, serve the community as the first Believers had done.

Our gift had been an act of faith. We believed that the Community was to be truly a community of mind and spirit dedicated to a single purpose. Perhaps we had set ourselves an impossible task. Man's ideals, it is said, often exceed his grasp.

THE SHAKER LIBRARY

June 1975

Early in our research it became apparent that in the documenting of our growing collection we would need the help of the Believers themselves. This came about quite naturally. Whenever time allowed

The Edward Deming Andrews Memorial Shaker Collection

Mrs. Andrews and her children, Ann Andrews Kane and David Volk Andrews at the dedication of the Shaker Library at the Henry Francis du Pont Winterthur Museum.

we were asked to "visit" and inquire further into the "why" of this or that. As our discussion progressed, a book, pamphlet or letter was brought forth to illustrate a point.

These treasures were the beginning of a new commitment—our Shaker library—the "sealing of a Joint Interest" as an Elder put it. It was indeed the heart of our work and through its use and growth we came to feel the strength and discipline of the Order. We felt, too, a responsibility for the future of the library equal to that of the early "caretakers."

As time went on in the development of our plans, we searched for the "perfect society" in which to entrust such a gift and traveled to many libraries here and abroad. In our contacts we found enthusiasm and advice and many promises to carry out our dream. The Shaker precept, "To possess as though you possessed not" took on a new and broader meaning. But we had become wary and decided for the time being to wait and work on our manuscripts.

Following Ted's death in June 1964 it became my responsibility to seek publication of the five remaining manuscripts. While I devoted myself to this effort, the concern as to the destination of the library never lessened. Inquiries as to its availability and future were many. A decision had to be made.

Then word came of the proposed new library at the Winterthur Museum. The ideals and achievements of Mr. Henry Francis du Pont, its founder, had been an inspiration to us. We had established a rapport with the staff when we collaborated on the installation of the Museum's Shaker rooms. This atmosphere of friendship and trust led to a clear decision.

Early in 1967 the search for the "perfect society" was ended and our library was prepared for its transfer to Winterthur. It was a joyous occasion. In November 1969 a symposium, "Aspects of Shaker Culture," was held marking the dedication of the Edward Deming Andrews Memorial Shaker Collection.

The fruits of the Shaker tree are still being gathered. The bounty we enjoy daily, sharing it with those who come and go. The collecting is virtually over, but the studying and evaluating go on. We learn from all who share our interest. Little did we realize when we stopped that day long ago to buy a loaf of Shaker bread that we were casting bread upon the waters.

The Shaker tree is a vital growth, bearing fruit in abundance. Gathering it into our homes, our books, and our lives has been a great adventure.

It is my privilege to publish here for the first time the Descriptive Catalogue written by Edward Deming Andrews of the Andrews gift to Shaker Community, Inc., in January 1964 of Shaker furniture, inspirational drawings, home, shop and farm industries, photographs by William F. Winter of Shaker friends, printed literature, manuscripts, stereographs, engravings, and architectural drawings, related particularly to the Hancock Shaker Community.

My hope is that through this medium, the scope and provenance of the collection will be fully defined and interpreted according to its "meaning and message."

F.A.

DESCRIPTIVE CATALOGUE

of the
EDWARD DEMING ANDREWS AND FAITH ANDREWS
SHAKER COLLECTION
at
HANCOCK (MASS.) VILLAGE

Preface

In any study or exhibition of the work of the American Believers, commonly called Shakers, it is essential that certain facts be kept in mind: first, that the culture was religious in foundation and perfectionist in spirit; secondly, that workmanship was a communal expression, the product of social rather than individual principles and tastes; and thirdly, that the purpose of all work done in the society was good use, "the good of man." This last concept was one rooted in medieval thought, when "art" was considered as "the making well, or properly arranging," of anything that needs to be made or arranged. "In the Middle Ages," wrote Maitre Minvielle, "the liberal arts and trades were . . . on a footing of equality, and in the language of that day they were often designated by the same words."

It is misleading, therefore, to think of Shaker "art" as aesthetics. Moreover it is irrelevant, in the present case, to draw a distinction between fine art and what is called applied or decorative. What we are concerned with is the skillful fashioning of material into forms which satisfied the conscience and ministered to the needs, both physical and spiritual, of a consecrate order. To understand the forces at work out of which the forms evolved is of central importance. Who were the

Shakers, what did they believe, what were they seeking in their work and worship?

In doctrinal terms, it was salvation, regeneration, a state of blessedness, which was the goal, indeed, of other religions. But with the Shakers the means were unorthodox: the celibate life, separation of the sexes, confession of sin, separation from the world, community of property—principles demanding self-denial, discipline under holy orders, cooperative labor. It was a straight and narrow way. But those who undertook it were convinced it was the only path to redemption, and in this spirit voluntarily gave up their possessions, their families and worldly concerns to consecrate themselves to a higher destiny.

Renunciation at the outset was followed by an affirmative program. Having repudiated selfish interests, the Believers channeled their energies into new courses, "laboring to make the way of God their own." Though the process might not be completed in this life, they sought that fullness of the spirit which would eventually be free of all earthly dross. Perfection of self and of society was, they believed, a realizable objective.

Such a philosophy had effectual implications in the fields of craftsmanship and industry. Ever present was the incentive to rise above the carnal plane. "We are not called to labor . . . to be like the world," Father Joseph wrote, "but to excel them in order, union and peace, and in good works—works that are truly virtuous and useful to man, in this life." Shaker journals are full of allusions to good works, order, neatness, cleanliness, uniformity, "good use." In seeking to excel in the products of shop and farm, the Believers were constantly experimenting, retaining what was best, casting out the second-rate—"halfway work"—finding in the simplest forms the most satisfactory answers. Even in their mode of worship they sought by daily practice to perfect their songs, dances and rituals.

The effect of principle was everywhere manifest. The communal way of life was exemplified in long trestle tables and benches, commodious chests of drawers and tailoring counters, built-in cupboards, the cooking arches in the kitchen, etc.—furnishings that served group requirements, the needs of families numbering sometimes over a hundred sisters and brethren. But pieces for personal or small group use—chairs, stands, stools, desks, small tables, and so on—were no less important in a household economy where each individual had prescribed rights and duties. All furniture was made for predetermined places and functions, and in the case of chairs and special use pieces, often for particular persons. No matter how humble its purpose, it was well used, for property was part of the United Inheritance. It belonged to the Church, an order that was millennial in scope. Had not Mother

Ann enjoined her people to "do your work as though you had a thousand years to live"?

The belief that the sexes should be separate yet equal in rights and responsibilities found particular expression in Shaker architecture. In the dwellings there was dual arrangement of entrance doors, hallways and retiring rooms. Meeting houses were built with a spacious room on the first floor for communal worship and retiring rooms on the second floor for the ministerial order of two elders and two eldresses. Shops and other out-buildings were planned with regard to the specific functions of the sexes. "Separation acts" controlled the relationships between brethren and sisters, inevitably leaving an impress on mores and workmanship. Reduced to practice, the seven moral principles of the society—duty to God, duty to man, separation from the world, practical peace, simplicity of language, right use of property, and a virgin life—affected conspicuously the domestic arts and folkways of the Believers.

It is seldom possible to fix more than an approximate date for given pieces of Shaker furniture and other articles. The "classic" period of craftsmanship was the first half of the nineteenth century. Before 1800 design was experimental, a transition from colonial styles, a searching for new forms more expressive of the Shaker ethos. After the middle of the century, and noticeably after the Civil War, when the strict "line of separation" between the society and the world was becoming obscured, craftsmanship became vitiated—corrupted is not too strong a term—by a taste for decoration or "fancy" which would not have been countenanced in the earlier period.

Ascription of date and provenance is complicated by the fact that all colonies in the East, influenced in the beginning by patterns set by the parent society at New Lebanon, tended towards the production of a uniform style in architecture, furniture and various accessories. It was the same in the West, where Union Village was a center of influence. There were, however, recognizable variations between the work of the East and the West as well as subtle ones within each region and between communities. As for dates, when a desired design was achieved, it would be retained for decades. "We find out by trial what is best," a spokesman of the sect explained, "and when we have found a good thing . . . we stick to it." Only when a craftsman, with pardonable pride, fixed the date or his name or initials on a piece is it possible to document it with certainty. On the other hand, the copious records of the society afford abundant evidence on such matters as the time buildings were raised, industries begun, "improvements" made, as well as the nature and conduct of all community enterprises.

In a few years the Shaker culture will have passed into American history, with no followers of the saintly Ann to put its aspirations in words. Only two small communities remain, totaling less than a dozen members. It is all the more important, therefore, that the preface to this catalogue of our gift include this message from a true Believer who had lived in Canterbury most of her life. In answer to a request she wrote:

> The epitome of the heritage bequeathed by the generations who have lived their life is the strong belief in the necessity of universal love for all mankind, the experience of the Sense of Presence, the conscious feeling of the Indwelling Christ, the Holy Spirit—call it what you will, the assurance of living in Eternity now; the confidence in the closeness of the other world and its invisible companionship; the knowledge that all this is attainable by anyone.
>
> Mother Ann Lee said, "Labor to feel the life of God in your inheritance, your treasure, your occupation, your daily calling. Attaining this, the whole world is full of God."

Since the people themselves may soon be gone, the challenge confronting those who propose to preserve, in historical museums, their heritage, is how to maintain the animus with which they put their hands to work. In the original prospectus outlining the purpose of Shaker Community, Inc. of Hancock, Massachusetts, we stressed the importance of not only preserving but vitalizing their contributions, both material and spiritual, of conserving not only the artifacts but the values of an unusually significant way of life and work.

Our present concern, as principal donors of the materials, is to so document our Collection that there will always be a faithful record of its content. That is our privilege and our responsibility—for only we, who collected the material in the first place and lived with it for many years, can document it with authority. The furniture and all the rest were part of our lives. We loved the things not only for their intrinsic excellence but also for their symbolic value as reminders of a people and a culture for which we had profound respect. We passed them on to the Community of Hancock in order that those who come after us might share our knowledge, our delight and our inspiration. That is their mission.

CATALOGUE

Plate numbers refer to illustrations in *Shaker Furniture, The Craftsmanship of an American Communal Sect,* Yale University, New Haven, 1937; reprinted: Yale 1939; Dover Publications, Inc., N.Y. 1950-1973. Page numbers refer to illustrations in the present volume.

1. LONG TRESTLE TABLE

Every meal was considered a sacrament, and instead of celebrating the Lord's Supper monthly or quarterly, as other Christians did, they celebrated it daily. (Marianne Finch. *An Englishwoman's Experience in America.* London, 1853.)

Such a piece, twenty feet long, could have been made only for *communal* use. It was found on the upper floor of the old grist mill of the West "lot" or family, a branch of the North family, New Lebanon, where for years it had been used in the preparation of pharmaceutical products. It may have been the original dining table at the North family, which was fully organized in 1814. Page 24.

Sisters and brethren ate at separate tables, in "squares" of four, with complete servings of food set beforehand for each group. A bell, or shell, was sounded a half hour before the meal, and another just before it was ready to be served. Then the family, led by the elders and eldresses, filed slowly into the refectory, knelt in silent prayer, took their places on the benches or chairs, then ate in silence. When the meal was over, at a signal from the presiding elder or eldress, they again knelt in prayer before departing for their various callings.

2. DINING BENCHES (2)

Benches were used as seats before the one and two slat chairs were made. These are ten feet long, pine, stained dark red. Plate 2.

3. TRUSTEES' DESK

The line of beauty is the result of perfect economy. (Emerson. *The Conduct of Life.*)

Every piece of Shaker furniture, once its origin is known, has a story to tell. If seen in a shop, it might still attract the attention of a collector of American antiques, if not the connoisseur. But when one knows the place where for a century or more it served a certain purpose, its intrinsic merit as a fine example of craftsmanship is enriched by the associations it evokes. It is no longer an isolated ob-

Trustees' desk

ject, an item for decoration, but one imbued with meaning stemming from the social, religious or economic background of those who made it for their own use.

When we first saw this desk it had been standing for many years in the corner of a room in an abandoned herb shop in the Center family or Second Order of the New Lebanon Church. The aged sister who sold it to us recalled that it was originally used by the trustees or deacons of that order. There were two trustees in each family, charged—in cooperation with the deacons—with the family's temporal affairs ("temporalities"). The two lids, the double set of drawers and cupboards, some still retaining labels for filing, bespeak the dual nature of Shaker social and economic organization—a quality that is reflected in the balanced design of much of the furniture and architecture. Plate 36.

The Second Order, in which the herb industry was concentrated at New Lebanon, was established as a separate family about 1811, a clue to the date when the desk was made. At this community, as in several other branches of the United Society, the preparation of medicinal herbs, barks, roots and flowers for the pharmaceutical market was a basic industry.

Table desk

4. SCHOOLROOM DESK WITH BENCH (SLAT BACK)

All work done, or things made, in the Church for their own use ought to be faithfully and well done, but plain and without superfluity. (Joseph Meacham. *Way Marks* 1791-1796.)

Like the long trestle table, this desk is an expression of communal practice. It illustrates, moreover, the Shaker sense of economy, the maximum utilization of space in a given piece. The six writing lids fold into the top when not in use. There are no unnecessary projections, at the sides or ends, beyond the skirt. The bench fits neatly underneath the desk. Page 68 and Plate 35.

The piece is the product of the period, beginning about 1817, when the Believers, always alert to improvements, adopted the Lancasterian or monitor method of teaching, with selected pupils passing on to a group the instructions of the teacher.

Shaker education, with three months of schooling for the boys in winter and three for the girls in summer, was limited and strictly utilitarian. However, as Barnabas Bates observed in *Peculiarities of the Shakers,** "where traits of uncommon genius appear, they have opportunities for instruction accordingly, and thus all receive instruction proportioned to their talents and capacities for usefulness."

5. TABLE DESK OR WRITING BOX

A characteristic example of Shaker craftsmanship, found in many communities, is the table desk (sometimes erroneously called a lap desk), made in a variety of forms, sometimes flat, sometimes slanting. Often, as here, there is a long shallow drawer which pulls out from one end. Sometimes a small drawer at the end is provided for an ink pot. Plate 38.

6. CANDLE OR ROUND STAND

In the unadorned placidity of these objects (one finds) a tangible revelation of the tranquil spirit that may accompany profound religious faith. (Homer Eaton Keyes, *The Magazine Antiques,* 1935.)

There are many types of candle stands. With few exceptions, the expanding curve of the post continues downward with no superfluous turning and terminates at the base with the convex or double arcs of the legs. The one at Shaker Community, Inc. is typical of New Lebanon Church craftsmanship. Plate 16.

Candle stand

7. PEG-LEG STAND

The stick leg or peg-leg stands are early pieces. They usually have, as here, a rectangular rimmed top and a drawer. Page 60 (second stand from left) and plate 12.

* Barnabus Bates, *Peculiarities of the Shakers,* New York, J.K. Porter, 1832, p. 46. The authorship of *Peculiarities of the Shakers* has been incorrectly attributed to Benjamin Silliman.

8. SEWING CABINET

All things ought to be made according to their order and use; and all things kept decent and in good order . . . (Meacham, *Way Marks.*)

One of a diversity of designs from the Hancock Shaker Community, the drop leaf at the back may be raised to extend the work surface. Plate 33 (left). Accessories for sewing cabinets, tables and stands included spool stands, often stained red or yellow, with a full complement of delicately turned spools.

In the creative period of Shaker culture the Believers were largely self-sufficient in supplying their domestic needs. This was notably true of their clothing: cloth and leather shoes, sisters' dresses and undergarments, socks, brethren's coats and clothes, kerchiefs and handkerchiefs, straw and beaver hats, palm-leaf bonnets, cloaks, surtouts, and so on. Each item was specifically prescribed as to use and appropriately marked with the initials of the user or the family. Spinning, weaving and the tailoring of sisters' garments fell within the province of the sisterhood, as did many other household and shop duties— such handicraft, for instance, as poplar basketry, the lining of oval boxes, the braiding of whiplashes, etc. One of the most common articles of furniture, therefore, was the sewing table, cabinet or stand, which—unlike the tailoring counters—were small, compact and intended for the use of only one or two sisters.

9. SEWING STAND

Made at Hancock Shaker Community. The exposure of the dovetailed drawer, which may be pulled out from either side for the convenience of two seamstresses, aptly illustrates a dictum of English art critic John Ruskin: The essential and necessary structure of an object should never be lost sight of nor concealed by secondary forms or ornament. Plate 15 (right).

10. SWIVEL CHAIR

The swivel chair or stool, sometimes called a "revolver," was a frequent accessory in the sewing rooms at New Lebanon. Plate 31 (left). Sometimes the spokes as well as the curved piece at the top were iron rods.

11. HIGH SWIVEL CHAIR

For shop use. Plate 48.

12. SPLAY LEG TABLE

In their search for the perfection of use, they were, after all, searching for perfection, and perfection is the supreme attribute of art. (Henry McBride, *The New York Times,* 1935.)

A sturdy table from the kitchen or buttery at Sabbathday Lake. Plate 9 (left).

13. DROP LEAF TABLE WITH STRETCHER BASE

The stretcher base table is an unusual early type, but not unique. Another one, used in a wash house and later in a cannery at New Lebanon, was published in the January 1933 issue of *The Magazine Antiques.* The one at Shaker Community, Inc. also came from New Lebanon. Plate 7.

Drop leaf table

14. DROP LEAF TABLE

Made at the Hancock Shaker Community. Plate 8 (right).

15. WASH BENCH

Strengthened by a medial stretcher projecting and fastened beyond the end boards. From the Second family, New Lebanon. Plate 10 (left).

16. WASH STAND

With swiveling disc for holding a slop vessel. Pine and maple. It came from the North family at New Lebanon.

17. DESK ON TRIPOD BASE
(DEACONESS'S DESK)

Made at the Hancock Shaker Community. The post leg is turned in a manner which the early Shakers would have called superfluous and is in that sense atypical. Plate 37.

Settee

18. SETTEE

Let it be plain and simple, of good and substantial quality, unembellished by any superfluities which add nothing to its goodness or durability. (Shaker tenet.)

A unique piece from the North family, New Lebanon, the novitiate or gathering order of that community. It was here that visitors from the world were received, and it was probably for the convenience of such inquirers, or travelers, that the settee was made.

19. HERB CUPBOARD WITH SILL

The nurse-shop at the North family, New Lebanon, was located on the second floor of the Second family dwelling. In one long narrow room brightly lighted by south windows, there were two identical cupboards to hold the medicinal herbs grown in the physic gardens and widely used in the Shaker infirmaries.

Herb Cupboard

Herb labels are pasted on the outside of the four deep drawers. The wood is butternut.

20. READING STAND WITH PEG LEGS

Tinted a thin pink wash. Acquired at an auction sale in New Lebanon and probably from the New Lebanon Church. It may have been used by the public preacher, F.W. Evans. A unique piece.

21. WALL CLOCK

The clock is an emblem of a Shaker community because everything goes on time...absolute punctuality is a *sine qua non* of a successful community. (*The Manifesto,* 1887.)

This clock was made at New Lebanon by Isaac N. Youngs and is dated 1840. Plate 42.

One cannot describe adequately any product of Shaker skill without seeing, in the mind's eye, its original placement and function. A clock is a good example of this—whether it be a tall floor clock at the end of a hallway used by the eldresses or deaconesses in charge of housework or a wall clock hanging in the kitchen or dining room which told the time for ringing the cupola bell for rising, meals, and retiring.

This was the usual schedule:

	Summer	Winter
Signal for rising	4:30 A.M.	5:30 A.M.
Call to breakfast	5:50	6:50
Breakfast	6:00	7:00
Call to dinner	11:50	11:50
Dinner	12 noon	12 noon
Call to supper	5:50 P.M.	5:50 P.M.
Supper	6:00	6:00
Signal for "retiring time"	7:30	8:00
Call to evening worship or union meeting	8:00	8:30
Close of day	9:00	9:30

Though occupations were diversified, with considerable flexibility of assignment, each day followed a set pattern of sleep, meals, labor and worship. It was necessary in such a tightly knit cooperative for the deacons, deaconesses and overseers to plan the work of each day, and to know where and when to find every member. Even in the great stone barn at New Lebanon North family there was a clock, and the cows were milked "exactly at fixed times."

22. WAG-ON-THE-WALL CLOCK

Probably an early product of Isaac N. Young's workshop. Plate 4.

Looking glass

Three-slat chair

23. LOOKING GLASS

One good looking glass, which ought not to exceed eighteen inches in length, and twelve in width, with a plain frame. (*Millennial Laws*, 1845.)

In Ann Lee's time, ornamented looking glasses were considered, no less than ear and finger rings, as instruments of worldly vanity. But the pragmatic Shakers came to recognize mirrors as acceptable means of promoting neatness and cleanliness. They were being made by 1821, if not before, and set in a rack (with a grooved base strip) which was suspended from the peg board. By means of a tape at the top, the mirror could be tilted to the desired angle. Often the base strip was fitted with small wooden or cast brass pegs or knobs on which brushes could be hung. Plate 30.

Cot

24. COT

The early cots or beds had rollers so that they could be conveniently moved when they were being made up by the sisters in the morning. Plate 40.

25. BREAD-CUTTING TABLE

Plate 10.

26. CHAIRS

These narrow, light-slatted, straight chairs are . . . almost too perfect, too economical in their performance of their function, like Euclid's "beauty bare." One does not need to know anything about the Shakers to know that here is a complete and final expression of the culture which produced it. (Elizabeth McCausland, *The Magazine of Art*, December 1944.)

a) One-slat chairs (2), Plate 3; b) Two-slat chairs (2), Plate 3; c) Three-slat chairs splint seats (2), Plate 4; d) Child's side chair, Plate 18; e) Child's rocking chair, Plate 18; f) Brethren's armed rocking chair, Plate 14; g) Sisters' armed rocking chair, Plate 30 (right); h) Sisters' sewing chair, Plate 15 (right); i) Two-slat high-seated shop chairs (2), Plates 11, 30; j) One-slat high-seated (splint) shop chair, Plate 46; k) Wagon chair; l) Sisters' armed rocking chair; m) Sisters' four-slat rocker mushroom, Plate 30.

As the only forms of craftsmanship in wood (with the exception of oval boxes and coopersware) to be sold to the world, Shaker chairs are relatively well known. The Believers were pioneers in an industry that began at New Lebanon in the late 1780's, continuing there for a century and a half. The first chairs were "common": three slat side-chairs, painted red or yellow or finished to expose the native wood. By 1800 the shop at the Hill or East family was also turning out a few

Wagon Chair

wagon chairs, "small" or "slipper" chairs, and "easy" or rocking chairs, the latter with or without arms. Following the example of the parent society, as they did in the case of the basic medicinal herb, garden seed and broom industries, many other Shaker communities began chair-making at an early period. Besides the types mentioned, production included dining chairs with one or two slats, turning chairs or stool chairs for sewing—the forerunners of our swivel chairs and chairs for special shop use. Occasionally the seats were made of cane, leather or rush, but a fine, narrow splint was the usual material. After the Civil War, hand-woven tapes of varied colors were used.

Shaker chairs are noted for their "strength, sprightliness and modest beauty"—to use the words of the diploma and bronze medal they received at the Philadelphia Centennial. Despite a variety of styles, there are common features which distinguish them from the colonial slatbacks: the slender lines of the posts, the graceful finials, the absence of all excess turnings, the natural finish, the seats of colored listing. The tilting chair was a particular type, so-called for the ball-and-socket buttons on the bottom of the back posts to allow the sitter to lean back without slipping or wearing the carpet. After the war, when a degree of standardization (and also outside competition) accompanied increased production, chairs and foot benches could be identified by catalogue number and a trademark in gold transfer.

Father Joseph Meacham, the American-born organizer of Shaker communitarianism, wrote in his *Way Marks* that "all things made in the Church should be made according to their order and use." Nothing illustrates this precept better than Shaker chairs. The first rockers were made for the comfort of the aged and infirm, for whom there was always the most solicitous concern. High-seated chairs for tailoring counters and work benches, swivel seats for sewing cabinets, loom stools, two-, three- and four-step stools to reach high cupboards or drawers, children's chairs, slipper chairs, chairs adapted to the physique of given users—all express the intimate coordination between the craftsmanship of the sect and its cultural, religious and economic background.

27. BENCHES

Under the generic name of "bench" may be listed many forms of Shaker craftsmanship with many uses. Long dining benches have been listed under No. 2. Benches were made for the school room desks (No. 4). Plate 35. A wash bench is noted in No. 15.

a) Two-step foot bench, Plate 27; b) Shoemaker's bench with tools, Page 140 and Plate 47; c) Shingle maker's bench; d) Apple coring bench; e) Benches with back rest but no arms (2); f) Splay-leg shop bench, Plate 48; g) Platform or "throne" for a chair. Used near window for better light.

28. STOOLS

a) Two-step stool, Plate 22; b) Foot stools or benches (3), Plates 7 and 15.

29. STOVES

We have a right to improve the inventions of man so far as is useful and necessary, but not to vainglory, or anything superfluous. (Joseph Meacham, *Way Marks*, 1791-1796.)

Shaker wood-burning stoves were an improvement in their function over the so-called "box stoves" made by the world. There was no ornamentation, no useless accessories. The little draft door was so contrived that the heat could be regulated within a few degrees of the desired temperature. By extending or angling the stovepipe, or by adding an upper chamber or deck, the mechanics obtained the maximum amount of radiation. Some stoves were equipped with a reservoir in which flatirons could be heated. The board on which the stove rested was a finishing touch, and when covered with tin or zinc, a safety measure.

a) Retiring room stove; b) Double deck stove; c) Early stove with large door, in ministry wash house; d) Stove patterns.

30. COOKING ARCH

Originally in the kitchen of the Hancock Shaker Community dwelling and now reinstalled there.

31. STOVE EQUIPMENT

a) Shovels, tongs and ash removers; b) Shovels, tongs.

32. WOOD BOX

With towel rack. Plate 21.

33. LIFT-TOP WOOD BOX

34. CHIP BOX

For kindling. Plate 21.

35. CUPBOARD

From shoemaker's shop, New Lebanon. Pine, painted red with four doors.

Oval boxes

36. OVAL BOXES (COLLECTION)

A perfect composition in itself, a completely realized unit of form. (Anon.)

Box-making was a project in the accomplishment of which the Shaker apprentice could learn how to plane, dovetail and stain. There was always a need for candle-boxes, squill boxes, pipe stem boxes, small storage boxes, chip boxes and the like.

The bentwood oval boxes, however, required greater skill. To make them so that the covers would fit snugly over, and the bottoms tightly within the oval bands, was precision work of the first order. The delicately cut "fingers" or wrappers, the range in sizes (thirteen in all, from the smallest to the largest), and the colors used in the finish (reds, yellows, greens, occasionally blue), distinguish the boxes from their crude colonial prototypes. Useful for many purposes—to hold herbs, seeds, dyes, pumice, small tools, tacks, buttons, spools, yarn, kerchiefs, etc., even hats and bonnets—they found their way into both the dwellings and shops, and were sold to the world as early as the 1790's. Plate 43.

37-50 INDUSTRIAL MATERIALS*

The historian . . . wants to know the truth about life, and he must take it where he finds it. It will not do for him to study only the highest artistic realizations of a period. Often he can learn more about the forces that shape its life from the common objects and utensils which are the undisguised products of its industries. (S. Giedion. *Space, Time and Architecture.*)

Though the Shaker economy, like that of other communitarian experiments in America, was based on agriculture and stock raising, it was distinct in that farming was supplemented by a complex industrial organization. Some of the shop activities, like blacksmithing and the mechanical trades, bore little direct relationship to the soil. But most—and this was the peculiar Shaker genius—were extensions of agricultural and horticultural pursuits, occupations in which the produce of the land, the herds, the woodlots and the quarries was processed into consumer goods for which there was home need and a ready market.

Note the nature of such industries: grist-milling, carpentry jobbing, shingle and brick making, tanning and manufacturing in leather, broom and brush making, the weaving, fulling and dyeing of cloth, tailoring, basketry, distilling, joinery, the garden seed industry, the medicinal herb industry, the dried sweet corn and dried apple industries, the "kitchen industries" (canning, pickling, preserving, etc.), and the manufacture of coopersware, buttons, whips, pipes and sieves. In all of these the Believers utilized the materials at hand. And in all, the emphasis was not on the returns but on "good use," work that would represent the ideals

---

* Further documentation and illustrations of the Shaker industries may be found in *Work and Worship, The Economic Order of the Shakers,* Edward Deming Andrews and Faith Andrews, New York Graphic Society, 1974, Greenwich, Conn.

Sisters' clothing

of a Christian society. Consequently the product had a widespread reputation and a premium price in the market.

All Shaker industries are represented in the Andrews Collection at Shaker Community, Inc.

37. TEXTILE (WEAVING)AND CLOTHING INDUSTRIES

One of the earliest Shaker industries was weaving. They spun their own wool and flax, wove, fulled and dyed their own cloth, and made their own reels, spinning wheels and looms.

The same pains were expended on occupational equipment as on the furnishings of the meeting-houses and dwellings. The turnings on the posts of clock-reels are as simple as those on tables and chairs, and one has the same type of snake feet as are found on candle stands. Page 215 and Plate 24 (right). Looms for weaving tape, straw and palm leaf were fashioned with the highest degree of "nicety" combined with strength. Rug and carpet looms, made of hard maple, have the same clean lines and finish as a chest of drawers.

Shaker textiles, including the dress of the sisters and brethren, have a distinct character, refuting the common idea that the Believers were indifferent to color and a certain style. True, the colors were low-keyed, and the use of such dyes as sumac, hemlock, butternut, copperas and indigo tended to sober effect. But, in general, the order was more concerned with uniformity than sobriety, and often, as in their madder-red fabrics, the silk kerchiefs woven in Kentucky and Ohio, and the sheen of their "dressed" cloth, the feeling for color and finish is abundantly evident. If the Shakers had completely outlawed the satisfaction of the senses, they would never have combined colors in braids, carpets and chair tapes, or introduced in their weaves such patterns as the check, diaper, diamond and stripe. The sisters' Sabbathday dress was an ethereal white.

a) Cloth loom. Made by Henry De-Witt, New Lebanon, 1834; b) Tape loom; c) Pleasant spinner; d) Hand cards; e) Reels, one with snake feet. Includes clock-reels; f) Table swifts; g) Scarns (3), includes one with spools; h) Swatches of cloth; i) Silk kerchiefs; j) Sisters' dresses and shoes; k) Brethren's clothes and shoes; l) Piece of Mother Ann's dress; m) Measuring sticks; n) Pressing boards; o) Flat irons and tailoring geese; p) Samples of thread, yarn and braid on spools; q) Tailoring shears; r) Pleat pressing tools; s) Woven rugs; t) Knitting needles in cases; u) Flax wheel; v) Hatchels, flax; w) Loom stools; x) Stand loom.

Hand cards

Table swift

Reels

Sisters' shoes

Brethren's clothes

38. HATTING AND BONNET MAKING

a) Bonnets (straw, palm-leaf and cloth); b) Bonnet and hat forms; c) Bonnet patterns (wood and tin); d) Net cap drying rack; e) Box containing net caps; f) Hat stretchers.

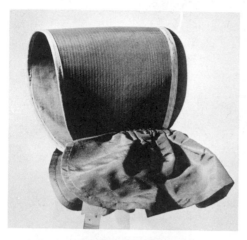

Palm-leaf bonnet covered with silk

39. POPLAR BASKETRY

We . . . bought some of their delicate baskets, in the manufacture of which the line of beauty has unconsciously introduced itself. (Amelia M. Murray, *Letters from the United States,* London, 1856.)

The delicate white poplar baskets made by the sisterhood were as distinctly Shaker as the oval boxes. After the thin poplar bands were cut (by a gauge called a straw-stripper) they were woven over small wooden molds, in various forms with names often suggestive of their use: box, knife, spoon, spoon "with ears," sugar bowl, flask, tub, demijohn, fruit, melon, saucer, cushion, card, round, hexigon, small hexigon, "kitten head" and "cat head." For sale or for use in the sewing rooms, oval boxes were frequently lined with colored silk and furnished with little baskets like the cushion, round and hexigon.

a) Poplar baskets (collection); b) Gauges for stripping poplar.

40. COOPERING

a) Dry measures, sealed and unsealed; b) Dipper; c) Pails; d) Tubs; e) Keeler; f) Firkins; g) Wooden bowls; h) Barrels; i) Spit boxes; j) Apple sauce buckets.

41. THE GARDEN SEED INDUSTRY

Starting at Niskeyuna (Watervliet), New Lebanon, Hancock and Enfield (Conn.), the garden seed industry spread to other communities to become one of the Shakers' most lucrative occupations. Pioneers in packaging seeds in small envelopes (priced at first at three cents each), they were also enterprising in distribution, supplementing the wholesaling of seeds with commission accounts and the route system—peddling them throughout the countryside in the picturesque one-horse wagons which were one of their own improvements. The pasting of the seed envelopes was the province of the sisterhood; the printing was done on a

Poplar baskets

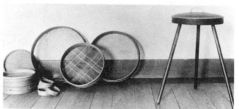

Sieves and sieve binder

Collection of coopers' ware

handpress; and the task of sorting seeds—for which special tables with rimmed tops were provided—was carried out periodically by the brethren with strictest care.

a) Garden bowls; b) Seed boxes; c) Sieves (wire and horse hair) for screening seeds; d) Sieve binder; e) Seed pails; f) Advertisement, broadside; g) Catalogues.

Cardboard containers, herb industry

42. THE MEDICINAL HERB INDUSTRY

Most colorful, perhaps, of all the Shaker industries was the one dealing with the cultivation and preparation of medicinal plants, barks, roots, seeds, flowers and "select powders" for the pharmaceutical trade. It forms a special chapter in the long history of herb growing, with its attendant folklore, its associations with fragrance, the color of flowers in garden and field, the aroma of good cooking. With the Believers, however, the "physics gardens" served primarily the cause of botanical medicine.

A few herbs—sage, summer savory, marjoram, thyme—were grown for culinary purposes. Some flowers, like the rose with its crimson petals, had a dual use, for rose water and the flavoring of apple pies. And though it was "contrary to order" to cultivate useless flowers, "fortunately for those of us who loved them," one sister admitted, "there are many plants which are beautiful as well as useful." Significantly, the labels used on herb packages and bottles were printed on brightly colored paper in shades of green, red, yellow, purple and brown.

a) Broadside advertisement, Enfield, Conn.; b) Labels (collection); c) Litho-

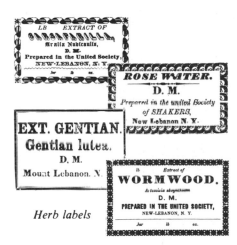

Herb labels

grapher's stone for printing labels; d) Vials, jars, bottles, cardboard containers (collection); e) Herb press (section); f) Medicinal herb room, New Lebanon (photograph); g) Herb cutters (collection); h) Herb drying rack; i) Herb label cabinet; j) Portable herb label rack; k) Pillmaker; l) Mortar and pestle. Pestle has ivory head; m) Mortar and pestle, wooden, small; n) Jar, brown crockery. Marked "G.K. Laurence, New Lebanon, N.Y."; o) Knife in frame.

Device for quartering apples

Baskets for domestic use

43. DRIED SWEET CORN INDUSTRY
a) Devices for stripping kernel from cob; b) Dried sweet corn containers; c) Advertisements.

44. APPLE SAUCE AND DRIED APPLE INDUSTRY
a) Knives; b) Corers; c) Apple quartering device; d) Advertisements.

45. BASKETS
For garden, farm and domestic use (collection).

46. CHEESE MAKING
a) Cheese press; b) Cheese rack.

47. BROOM AND BRUSH MANUFACTURE
a) Brooms, mops, etc. (collection); b) Brushes (collection).

48. CARPENTRY
a) Carpenters' tools (collection); b) Pattern makers' patterns; c) Measuring sticks.

49. WASH HOUSE (LAUNDRY) ACCESSORIES
a) Clothes carriers; b) Clothes racks; c) Clothes tubs; d) Dye tub; e) Dry sink.

50. FARMING
Collection of farm implements.

Collection of mops and brooms

Collection of cleaning, scrubbing and clothes brushes

Sieves, silk and hair

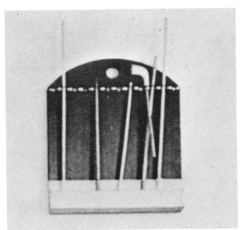

Pipe rack with clay pipe, bowls and stems

Electrostatic machine

51. Utilitarian objects—
A MISCELLANY

For years men have tried to divide art into two branches, calling one "fine" and the other "industrial," each incapable of surviving in such isolation. The wish, no doubt, was to make us believe that the "industrial" arts were so soiled by the degradation of labor that they could not enter the regions of pure beauty, as though beauty did not draw from materials its only outward form. (Anatole France. *Vers les temp meilleurs.*)

Just as a single detail may reveal quality in craftsmanship, so may the most commonplace tool, or its product, exemplify the medieval doctrine of good use. The following selection of tools, utensils and small handicraft illustrates not only the scope of Shaker industry but also the meticulous care expended on even the humblest items in the sect's economy.

a) Staff pen and ruler. Used in manuscript hymnals; b) Pipe rack, with clay pipe bowls and stems, Plate 14; c) Pipe plane; d) Pipe molds; e) Sieves, silk and hair; f) Shoemaker's candle stand, adjustable, Page 140 and Plate 47; g) Mitten mender, with detachable thumb piece; h) Glove menders; i) Whip lashes; j) Compass; k) Mortar and pestle; l) Wall rack or sconce for two candlesticks, candle missing, Plate 33; m) Lantern in wooden frame, Plate 48; n) Towel rack, Plate 40; o) Footwarmer, butternut, Plate 20; p) Small wall cupboard, New Lebanon, Plate 13; q) Clothes hangers (collection); r) Tinware (collection); s) Kitchen utensils. Collection includes dough trough, scoops,

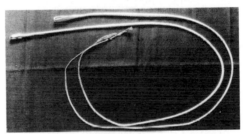
Whip lashes

Collection of tinware

Shaker wash mill

219

spoons (wooden), skimmers, vegetable trays, paddles or stirrers, bread boxes, berry boxes; t) Hanging cupboard or "safe"; u) Pie board rack; v) Knife holder, Plate 10; w) Hanging bookrack, Page 68 and Plate 35; x) Device for teaching time, Page 68 and Plate 35; y) Electrostatic machine, Plate 39; z) Model of Shaker "wash mill" (or washing machine); a-1) Dust box; a-2) Phrenological head (plaster); a-3) Bed cord tighteners; a-4) Schoolroom slates; a-5) Leather pocketbook; a-6) Sand shakers; a-7) Candle box; a-8) Candelabra, tin. From Tyringham meeting-house; a-9) Bookrack, Plate 37; a-10) "Adult cradle"; a-11) Office signs (2), trustees' office; a-12) "Lilly" for carrying off fumes from lamps; a-13) Hanging towel rack, Plate 6.

52. INSPIRATIONAL DRAWINGS AND PAINTINGS*

These emblematic designs are so uncommon and underivative that in the field of the religious arts they have no recognized place. The term "spirit drawings," sometimes used, carries the erroneous implication that they were automatic in execution. But they were inspired by visions and revelations, and so may be properly called "inspirational."

They belong to a single brief period in Shaker history, 1839-1859, the so-called "Era of Manifestations," when the order experienced an extraordinary revival of its early religious enthusiasm. Beginning among a group of children at Watervliet, N.Y., in 1837, the manifestations—marked by trances, visions and messages from the "heavenly sphere"—spread to all of the societies, east and west, growing more rapturous and mystical until they reached their climax in the early forties, when meetings were closed, and wooden crosses (see Chapter V) erected in front of the church warned visitors away. By 1845, however, public worship was renewed, and two years later the wave of spiritualism had virtually spent its force.

One phenomenon of the period was the composition of "gift songs," supposedly learned in vision and sometimes called extra songs, being sung in addition to the traditional hymns, anthems and dance songs of the order. Accompanying these were many new forms of exercise or laboring rituals. Other manifestations were the drawings, the first of which, appearing in 1839, were cryptic designs called "sacred sheets." Following these abstractions were small paper cut-outs, exquisitely inscribed with homiletic messages, in the form of hearts, fans and leaves (from the tree of life)—sometimes adorned with simple symbols: crowns, trumpets, lamps, doves, altars, musical instruments, etc. The more elaborate designs, in which color came to be used, began to appear in 1845, when the revival had reached its zenith. Then strangely enough, as the movement subsided, and for years after it had ceased altogether, the drawings grew in number, complexity of content, and artistry. What had begun as a graphic compulsive phase of mysticism developed, in the aftermath of the "awakening," into deliberate attempts to express its significance. It may be that time was needed to assimilate the experience.

Little was said about these drawings by the Shakers themselves. There is a veiled reference in "A Closing Roll" (Canterbury, 1843), written by the inspired seedsman, Philemon Stewart, who observed that such gifts "have been sent forth in this degree of nearness and semblance of natural things that do exist on earth, that you might be better able to appreciate in lively colors, and thrilling sensations, the real adornings and beauties of the spiritual world." Another allusion appears in Isaac N. Young's *A Concise View of the Church of God and of Christ, on Earth* (New Lebanon, 1856, (Manuscript) where the author refers to the "many notices to individuals this year past [1843] as before, in writing, with many drawings, signs and figures of objects in the spirit world, with mysterious writings, etc. which will, it is said at some future time be revealed and explained."

That is all. If the Shakers themselves could not explain them, all we can do is

---

* The Andrews collection of 14 Inspirational Drawings are among those illustrated and analyzed in their book, *Visions of the Heavenly Sphere, A Study of Shaker Religious Art.* Published for the Henry Francis du Pont Winterthur Museum by the University Press of Virginia, 1969, Charlottesville, Virginia.

to present a hypothesis. We do know, from eyewitness accounts, that participants in the exercises of the period were often swept by unusual fervor; that in a state of trance they had visions of heavenly glories; that the "departed spirits" of Mother Ann and other saints, as well as the spirits of Indians, Negroes, Eskimos, etc. so dominated their subconscious selves that they spoke and behaved like people truly possessed; and finally, that they received messages and songs that were documented by witnesses, and spiritual presents realistically described by the visionaries themselves. Occult influences were undeniably at work. Spirits were said to "move the hands" of the artists. Much is inexplicable. But so deeply did the manifestations penetrate the communal consciousness that one can understand the urge to record them in meaningful line and color.

In technique, content and color the Shaker inspirationals are unrelated, as noted, to any other forms of primitive or folk art. The artists often employed a sort of asymmetrical balance in their compositions, in the simple trees of life as well as the more elaborate representations. All are rich in symbolism; some motives being literal renderings of familiar objects (fans, lamps, tables, crowns, etc.) and natural forms (leaves, flowers, trees, the sun and moon, etc.), while others are purely imaginative, abstract, or intentionally decorative—though often identified by an inscription. In the colored designs the tints employed distinguish them from other indigenous folk art: the blues, greens, lambent yellows and bright pinks are clearer and more delicate than the colors in Pennsylvania Fraktur, for instance, or illuminated genealogies—as though the limners were inspired to emulate the hues of heaven.

Often these designs were bestowed by the artist on a Shaker brother or sister, an elder or eldress, as rewards or tokens of love and carefully put away as cherished mementos of an exalted experience. It was "contrary to order" to frame them and hang them on the walls, and in years after, in dread of misunderstanding or ridicule, most of them were destroyed.

List of inspirational drawings and paintings in the Collection. (The dimensions given here are those of the original sheets of paper.)

a. *Heart Gifts, or Rewards.* New Lebanon, 1844. Ink; 4 11/16 x 4 11/16, 4 x 4 1/16, 4 x 4 1/16, 3 15/16 x 4 inches

b. *The Tree of Light or Blazing Tree.* Hancock, 1845. Ink and water color; 18 1/8 x 22 9/32 inches

c. *From Holy Mother Wisdom to Sarah Ann Standish.* New Lebanon, 1847. Ink; 9 13/16 x 7 7/8 inches

d. *From Holy Mother Wisdom. To Eldress Dana or Mother.* Hancock, 1848. Ink and water color; 9 25/32 x 7 23/32 inches

e. *Mother Ann's Word to her little child Elizabeth Cantrell.* New Lebanon, 1848. Ink and water color; 7 1/2 x 7 1/2 inches

f. *A Type of Mother Hannah's Pocket Handkerchief.* New Lebanon, 1851. Ink and water color; 14 3/32 x 17 1/16 inches

g. *Floral Wreath. This Wreath Was Brought by Mother's Little Dove.* Hancock, 1853. Ink and water color; 12 1/16 x 11 15/16 inches

h. *A Gift from Mother Ann to the Elders at the North Family.* Hancock, 1854. Ink and water color; 19 x 12 inches

i. *A Bower of Mulberry Trees.* Hancock, 1854. Ink and water color; 18 1/8 x 23 1/16 inches

j. *An Emblem of the Heavenly Sphere.* Hancock, 1854. Ink and water color; 23 3/4 x 18 5/8 inches

k. *The Tree of Life.* Hancock, 1854. Ink and water color; 18 1/8 x 23 5/16 inches

l. *Heavenly Tree.* Hancock, 1855. Ink and water color; 23 5/16 x 18 1/8 inches

m. *Basket of Apples.* Hancock, 1856. Ink and water color; 10 1/8 x 8 3/16 inches

n. *A Tree of Love, a Tree of Life.* Hancock, 1857. Ink and water color; 9 7/16 x 9 3/16 inches

53. ARCHITECTURAL MATERIALS

Pegboard, doors, mouldings, window casings, hardware, etc., from the meeting room of the original Hancock Shaker meeting-house which was demolished in 1937.

54. LEDGERS, DAYBOOKS, ETC.

55. PRINTED LITERATURE

a) *The Testimony of Christ's Second Appearing,* Albany, 1810; b) *Millennial Praises,* Hancock, 1813; c) Files of *The Shaker, Shaker and Shakeress* and *The Manifesto;* d) Leaves from Eads' book on tailoring.

56. MANUSCRIPTS

a) Herb journal of Elisha Myrick, Harvard community; b) Letter from James Whittaker to Josiah Talcott, Ashfield; c) Examples of indentures and discharge; d) Record sheet of old cheese house, Elvira Hulett, Hancock, 1849; e) A Journal Concerning Bees in the Second Order; f) Manuscript hymnal.

57. ARCHITECTURAL DRAWINGS

Related to the early Hancock Shaker Community.

58. STEREOGRAPHS (COLLECTION)

59. DRAWINGS BY A. BOYD HOUGHTON

In 1870, following Elder Frederick Evans' proselytizing mission to England, *The London Graphic* commissioned A. Boyd Houghton to do a series of drawings of the American Shakers.

a) *Ring Dance;* b) *Shaker Evans at Home;* c) *The Gift of Love, Evening Meeting;* d) *Solemn March, The Final Procession.*

60. WOOD ENGRAVING BY JOSEPH BECKER

Singing Meeting, from Frank Leslie's *Popular Monthly,* December, 1885.

61. PHOTOGRAPHS BY WILLIAM F. WINTER

a) Sister Sadie Neale; b) Eldress Emma Neale; c) Eldress Sarah Collins; d) Eldress Anna Case; e) Eldress Fannie Estabrook; f) Brother Ricardo Belden; g) Evaporating room, Herb House, New Lebanon.

62. COLOR PRINT

Pressing and packaging herbs.

Therefore our labor is to do good, in our day and generation, to all men, as far as we are able, by faithfulness and frugality in the works of our hands.
—Shaker Memorial, 1816